WHITEHEAD'S ORGANIC PHILOSOPHY OF SCIENCE

WHITEHEAD'S
ORGANIC PHILOSOPHY
OF SCIENCE

Ann L. Plamondon

State University of New York Press • Albany • 1979

Whitehead's Organic Philosophy of Science
First Edition

Published by State University of New York Press
Albany, New York 12246

Copyright © 1979 State University of New York

Composed by
Typography Services
Loudonville, New York 12211

Printed in the United States of America

Library of Congress Cataloging in Publication Data

Plamondon, Ann L.
Whitehead's organic philosophy of science.

Includes bibliographical references.
1. Science—Philosophy.   2. Metaphysics.
3. Whitehead, Alfred North, 1861-1947.   I. Title.
Q175.P564   192   78-7350
ISBN 0-87395-166-2

Contents

CONTENTS

Abbreviations

The following are the abbreviations of titles and the editions of White-head's writings used in text references.

AI ADVENTURES OF IDEAS, New York, The Macmillan Co., 1956.

CN THE CONCEPT OF NATURE, Cambridge, Cambridge University Press, 1920.

FR THE FUNCTION OF REASON, Boston, Beacon Press, 1929.

ICNV "Indication, Classes, Numbers, Validation," ESSAYS IN SCIENCE AND PHILOSOPHY, New York, Philosophical Library, 1947.

MC "On Mathematical Concepts of the Material World," reprinted in ALFRED NORTH WHITEHEAD: AN ANTHOLOGY, Selected by F.S.C. Northrop and Mason W. Gross, New York, The Macmillan Co., 1953.

MT MODES OF THOUGHT, New York, Capricorn Books, 1958.

OT THE ORGANIZATION OF THOUGHT, EDUCATIONAL AND SCIENTIFIC, London, Williams and Norgate, 1917.

PM PRINCIPIA MATHEMATICA (with Bertrand Russell), 3 vols, Cambridge, Cambridge University Press, 1910-1913; second edition, 1925-1927.

PNK AN ENQUIRY CONCERNING THE PRINCIPLES OF NATURAL KNOWLEDGE, Cambridge, Cambridge University Press, 1919; second edition, 1925.

PR PROCESS AND REALITY, New York, The Macmillan Co., 1929.

S SYMBOLISM, New York, Capricorn Books, 1927.

SMW SCIENCE AND THE MODERN WORLD, New York, The Macmillan Co., 1950.

RM RELIGION IN THE MAKING, New York, The Macmillan Co., 1926.

Introduction

Three periods in the development of Whitehead's thought are generally recognized:[1]

(1) 1891-1913: The period of the writing of *Universal Algebra, Principia Mathematica,* and the memoir "On Mathematical Concepts of the Material World." During this period Whitehead's primary concerns were the problems of mathematics and of mathematical physics.

(2) 1914-1923: The period of the writing of *An Enquiry Concerning the Principles of Natural Knowledge, The Concept of Nature,* and *The Principle of Relativity, with Applications to Physical Science.* These works are considered to be Whitehead's most important contributions to the philosophy of physical science.[2]

(3) 1924-1947: The period of the writing of *Science and the Modern World, Process and Reality,* and *Adventures of Ideas.* These works constitute the fulfillment of Whitehead's hope expressed in the Preface to the second edition of *Principles of Natural Knowledge* that he would "in the immediate future . . . embody the standpoint of these volumes [of 1914-1923] in a more complete metaphysical study." Whitehead termed the metaphysical system he developed in these three late works "the philosophy of organism."

There is no general agreement with respect to the relationship of the doctrines Whitehead put forward during these three periods. Although all interpreters of Whitehead recognize a development and expansion of his ideas, there is a continuum of interpretation with respect to whether or not the development and expansion resulted in doctrines in the third period which are different in kind rather than degree from those of the first two periods. At one extreme it is held that the metaphysics of the third period differs only in degree from the premetaphysical concepts of the first two periods. In discussing the importance of the memoir "On Mathematical Concepts of the Material World," Mays maintains that discussions in *Process and Reality* cover problems beyond those explicitly considered in the early work but hold essentially the same philosophical solution:

1

> Whitehead here [MC] attempts to apply the axiomatic method to physical science. It is interesting to note that his account of a many-termed relation and its field, the entities related by it—in this case physical lines of force—bears a strong similarity to his account in *Process and Reality* of a general system of order permeated by electro-magnetic events. The change in Whitehead's view would not, then, seem to be as radical as has usually been supposed, since in some ways he might be said to be returning to his 1906 position. The Royal Society paper probably gives a much clearer insight into Whitehead's later philosophy than the many analogues that have been drawn between his work and such philosophers as Plato.[3]

This view is also held by Lawrence.[4] The evidence for this interpretation is that there seems to be a continuity in Whitehead's thought which consists of a development of the notions of the first period. Further, Whitehead does discuss the earlier problems in terms of the metaphysical scheme of the third period.

Other commentators maintain that only regarding a few doctrines is there a difference in kind with respect to the doctrines of the metaphysical period and those of the earlier periods. The two periods generally at issue are the second and third. The principal concern is the relationship of the earlier philosophy of science to the metaphysics of *Process and Reality.* Lowe writes: "His general philosophy of science cannot without distortion be separated from his metaphysics, and should never be evaluated on the lazy assumption that it is entirely contained in the books of 1919 to 1922, which he devoted exclusively to the philosophy of science."[5] Yet in discussing the transition from the works on the philosophy of science to the beginning of the centrality of the concept of "organism" in *Science and the Modern World,* Lowe does not emphasize a difference in kind in the fundamental doctrines of the two periods. "The 'organic theory of nature' is readily reached from the position of the 1920 books by thinking of their 'percipient event' as a temporal process with an internal constitution and making the following steps."[6] Lowe then lists and describes ten steps of transition which constitute developments from the 1920 books and which differ in degree from the notions contained in these works.

Palter seems to hold a view which is close to that of Lowe's.

> . . . while doing philosophy of science it is possible to ignore certain large metaphysical issues; and, though the converse is certainly not true (science being a vital datum for metaphysics), the results of an independent and prior

analysis of science may be incorporated without essential change in the developed metaphysical system. On the other hand, certain types of philosophical considerations, traditionally termed "metaphysical," do bulk large in Whitehead's philosophy of science; moreover, special adjustments in the philosophy of science are required when it is incorporated within the metaphysical system of Whitehead's "philosophy of organism."[7]

The special adjustments have mainly to do with the earlier view of the method of extensive abstraction and the modification of that doctrine in *Process and Reality*. The differences in the two doctrines will be discussed in sections 2 and 3, where it will be argued that the change in Whitehead's view does not amount to a new metaphysical doctrine.

At the opposite extreme of May's interpretation is that of Leclerc.[8] Leclerc maintains that Whitehead was not dealing with the same problems in *Process and Reality* as he was in the works of the second period. In the earlier works Whitehead was concerned with the new philosophical problems of science which had arisen with the developments in physics at the beginning of the twentieth century. Although the same problems receive discussion in *Process and Reality*, Leclerc believes they are not central. What is central in *Process and Reality* is the working out of traditional metaphysical problems. Leclerc interprets Whitehead's attempt "to *embody* the standpoint" of the philosophy of science in "a more complete metaphysical study" to mean that the metaphysics is not a mere development and extension of the philosophy of science; rather the metaphysics was concerned with a new set of problems and the investigation into these problems involved alteration of the earlier theories—an alteration in kind and not merely in degree.[9]

> . . . in turning to metaphysics Whitehead turned to a new set of problems, different from those which had previously been his primary concern. The result of this new preoccupation was by no means to leave his earlier theories unaltered. Their "embodiment" involved in the end a much more considerable change in Whitehead's theories about the problems of science than he himself had at first anticipated, and than most commentators have subsequently allowed.[10]

Palter has written the only book-length work on Whitehead's philosophy of science. We have seen that although he recognizes certain changes in Whitehead's philosophy of science to be entailed in the transition to the metaphysical works, his view of Whitehead's work is one of essential continuity. Consequently in discussing the philosophy of nature and its relationship to the philosophy of science, Palter adheres to the categories of the second period.[11] These categories may be illustrated by Whitehead's discussions in *The Concept of Nature*. There he sets out the function of a philosophy of science.

> The primary task of a philosophy of natural science is to elucidate the concept of nature, considered as one complex fact for knowledge, to exhibit the fundamental entities and the fundamental relations between entities in terms of which all laws of nature have to be stated, and to secure that the entities and relations thus exhibited are adequate for the expression of all the relations between entities which occur in nature (CN 46).

The fundamental entities of nature are not material particles in simple location (the Newtonian view), but "events" and "objects." "Events" is a category to account for change in nature. The essential relatedness of events is guaranteed by the extension of any event over other events (CN Ch. IV). "Objects" account for the permanence in nature. Whitehead considers the most important "objects" for philosophy of science to be sense objects, perceptual objects, and scientific objects (CN Ch. VII). The fundamental method for defining the spatio-temporal entities which constitute the subject matter of natural science (e.g., points and lines) from the fundamental entities is the method of extensive abstraction,[12] which will be discussed in sections 2 and 3.

If Palter's interpretation of the relation of the second and third periods of Whitehead's writings is correct, then his book stands as a definitive statement on the significance of Whitehead's doctrines for the philosophy of science. However it is a premise of this work that Palter's interpretation is incorrect and that his excellent book represents only that which can be drawn from Whitehead's writings of 1914-1923, which bears relevance to only a part of the discussions in contemporary philosophy of science.

This work assumes that Leclerc has correctly interpreted the relationship of the earlier philosophy of science to the later philosophy of organism and that the "considerable change in Whitehead's theories about the problems of science" has yet to be elucidated. It is the purpose of the present work to set out passages from Whitehead's philosophy of organism in order to elaborate the philosophy of nature embodied in the metaphysics and to draw the implications of the metaphysics for present discussions in the philosophy of science.

4

Part One will discuss the development of such concepts as points and lines and the method of extensive abstraction by means of which they are derived. Since Whitehead's thought began with problems of mathematics, the discussion will concentrate on points and lines as mathematical entities. In order to show the change in metaphysical view throughout the three periods, the question which will be raised will be that of the ontological status of these mathematical entities. Part Two will develop the categories of Whitehead's "organic" philosophy of science which replace the categories of "event" and "object" which were the foundational concepts of the philosophy of nature in the second period. Part Three will apply the categories developed in Part Two and the metaphysical implications of these categories to the discussion of laws, induction, explanation, conceptual change, and reduction in the current literature in the philosophy of science in the English-speaking world. Insofar as this work is successful in its task, it will show that Whitehead's contributions to the philosophy of science are greater than have previously been recognized. In addition it will show a continuity between metaphysics and the philosophy of science which has been largely neglected for the past five decades.

Part One

THE DEVELOPMENT OF WHITEHEAD'S THOUGHT

I. Geometry

1. The thesis of the first period

In all periods of his thought Whitehead was concerned with the foundations of geometry; in particular he was concerned with the definition of geometrical entities such as points and lines. One can distinguish three distinct periods in the development of Whitehead's conception of these entities. The first period is represented by the early memoir MC. Whitehead states the purpose of the memoir to be "the possible relations to space of the ultimate entities which (in ordinary language) constitute the 'stuff' in space" (MC 11). The investigation begins with certain definitions and goes on to outline five mathematical concepts of the material world. For each concept Whitehead considers one of the fundamental tasks to be the elucidation of the essential relation R, which holds between a definite number of entities, and of the "field" of R, or the class of entities between sets for which R holds. Once these entities which compose the field of R have been defined, one may go on to select the set of axioms, definitions, and resulting propositions which determine that particular concept of the material world. This latter task, however, is beyond the scope of our discussion. We will proceed by stating those definitions most relevant to our discussion and by briefly summarizing each of the five concepts. Then we will draw what seem to be the implications for the ontological status of geometrical entities involved in these concepts.

The following definitions are significant for understanding the meaning Whitehead attributes to "points" and "lines" in his subsequent discussions of the concepts of the material world.

> Definition.—The *Material World* is conceived as a set of relations and of entities which occur as forming the 'fields' of these relations.
> Definition.—The *Fundamental Relations* of the material world are those relations in it, which are not defined in terms of other entities, but are merely particularized by hypotheses [axioms] that they satisfy certain propositions . . .

9

Definition. — The complete class of those entities, which are members of the fields of fundamental relations, is called the class of *Ultimate Existents*. This technical name is adopted without prejudice to any philosophic solution of the question of the true relation to existence of the material world as thus conceived.

Every concept of the material world must include the idea of time. Time must be composed of *Instants*. . . . Thus *Instants* of Time will be found to be included among the ultimate existents of every concept.

Definition. — The class of ultimate existents, exclusive of the instants of time, will be called the class of *Objective Reals* (MC 13).

Concepts I, II, and III are "punctual" concepts. That is to say, the members of the field of the essential relation R, or the ultimate existents, are points (or particles, or both) — with the exception that some members of the field of R are to be conceived as instants of time. Lines and planes on the punctual concepts are, then, considered to be classes of points.

The class of objective reals for Concept I has two members, "points of space" and "particles of matter." The essential relation R is triadic and its field is the points of space. "R; *(abc)* means *the points a, b, c are in the linear order (or the R-order) abc*" (MC 25). This conception of space as composed of points applies only to an "unchanging world of space." In order to apply this concept of space to a changing world, one must take into account the other class of entities which compose the class of objective reals, *viz.*, particles of matter and also the class of extraneous triadic relations which hold between (1) a particle, (2) a point of space, and (3) an instant of time. Now the fact that the field of each extraneous relation possesses one and only one particle requires the postulation of as many extraneous relations as there are particles (MC 29).

Concept II differs from Concept I by its rejection of particles as members of the class of objective reals. Concept II retains only points of space as objective reals and considers the extraneous relations to be dyadic relations between points of space and instants of time (MC 29).

Concept II introduces the notion that points move. The class of objective reals is composed of moving points. The essential relation R is tetradic. R relates three objective reals and an instant of time. "R; *(abct)* may be read as stating the *objective reals a, b, c are in the R-order abc at the instant t*" (MC 30). The attribution of motion to points allows the points to perform the function of both the particles and the points of

Concept I. At any particular instant the objective reals may be conceived as the points of Concept I, and the geometry defined by the definitions and axioms of Concept I holds for Concept III with slight modifications. However, considered at another instant, the points will not stand in the same geometrical relations as they did at the previous instant. Then the objective reals considered in different states at different instants take on the character of the particles of Concept I (MC 30). Concept III has considerable advantage over Concepts I and II in that it avoids the assumption of the indefinitely many extraneous relations required by these concepts. Concept III requires only one extraneous relation to make possible the comparison of straight lines and planes at different instants (MC 31).

Concepts IV and V are "linear" concepts. For our purposes they may be treated as a single concept; we will only need to mention the principal respect in which they differ. On the linear concepts the members of the field of the essential relation R, with the exception of instants of time, are lines or, more precisely, are "single indivisible entities" which have properties generally associated with lines of force, except that they are endless. Linear objective reals are, thus, to be distinguished from geometrical lines, i.e., lines of points (MC 33). Just as on the punctual concepts lines are conceived to be classes of points, on the linear concepts points are conceived to be classes of linear objective reals. As complex entities the points of Concepts IV and V are capable of disintegration. We have seen in Concept III that the points of a particular instant are considered as different from the points of the previous instant in the sense, and only in the sense, that they have different relations. The linear concepts go one step further and maintain that the points of a particular instant are different from the points of the previous instant in the sense that they *are different entities;* that is to say, on the linear concepts, points do not persist from one instant to the next (MC 33). The essential relation R common to both Concepts IV and V is pentadic. R asserts the ordered intersection of three objective reals b, c, d by a fourth objective real a at an instant of time t. "The proposition R; *(abcdt)* can be read as the statement that the *objective real a intersects the objective reals b, c, d in the order bcd at the instant t*"(MC 34). The essential difference between Concepts IV and V is to be found in their respective definitions of points. On Concept IV geometrical points are

11

interpoints ("intersection-points" of linear objective reals), whereas on Concept V interpoints are merely "portions of points," and the definition of geometrical points requires the theory of dimensions in addition to the theory of interpoints (MC 35-39; 44-60).

The ontological implications for geometrical entities of Concepts I-V is not at all clear. Whitehead explicitly states that this memoir is primarily of mathematical interest and that the relation of these concepts to existence is not at issue. However in the preface of the memoir Whitehead does speak of an indirect relation of the inquiry to the philosophical issue.

> The general problem is here discussed purely for the sake of its logical (i.e., mathematical) interest. It has an indirect bearing on philosophy by disentangling the essentials of the idea of a material world from the accidents of one particular concept. The problem might, in the future, have a direct bearing upon physical science if a concept widely different from the prevailing concept could be elaborated, which allowed of a simpler enunciation of physical laws (MC 11-12).

Further, Whitehead's concluding remarks seem directly relevant to the above passage.

> What is wanted at this stage is some simple hypothesis concerning the motions of objective reals and correlating it with the motion of electric points and electrons. From such a hypothesis the whole electro-magnetic and gravitational laws might follow with the utmost simplicity. The complete concept involves the assumption of only one class of entities as forming the universe. Properties of 'space' and of the physical phenomena 'in space' become simply the properties of this single class of entities (MC 82).

In this memoir Whitehead set out to determine what could be the relations to space of the ultimate existents which constitute the "stuff" of space. These ultimate existents are conceived to be "essential features" of every concept of the material world, quite independently of the peculiarities of any one concept. Further, if one takes seriously Whitehead's concluding remarks, these ultimate existents are to be conceived as forming the universe, i.e., as *actualities*. We have seen that on the punctual concepts, these entities which constitute the "stuff" of space, i.e., the ultimate existents, include geometrical points. On the linear concepts the ultimate existents are "linear objective reals"; geometrical points and geometrical lines as classes of geometrical points are features of classes of these ultimate existents. Thus it seems that in this early memoir, Whitehead is conceiving geometrical entities to be ultimate existents or features of ultimate existents, hence to be features of actuality in a very important respect.

2. The thesis of the second period

Already in MC Whitehead saw very clearly that instants of time must be included among the ultimate existents. Each of the concepts of the material world which have been considered above involves the relating of an instant of time to members of a class or classes of objective reals. We have also seen that in the concluding remarks of this memoir, Whitehead maintains that the development of Concept V, which appears to have the greatest physical possibilities, would require the assumption of a single class of entities as forming the universe, i.e., as the class of ultimate existents. I take Whitehead to mean that the entities which would form the class of ultimate existents would include the concept of time as part of their intrinsic nature. Hence the distinction of a class of objective reals from the class of ultimate existents would be unnecessary: the objective reals would include the concept of time and hence would be the ultimate existents. Whitehead achieved the coherent introduction of time into his conception of the ultimate existents by turning to conceive the ultimate existents as events. Events are spatio-temporal; that is to say, events have both a temporal and a spatial extensiveness. This new conception of the nature of the ultimate existents as spatially and temporally extended events is representative of the second period in the development of Whitehead's thought.

During this period Whitehead came to accept the relational theory of space. This theory states that space is to be conceived as "a complex of relations between things" (PNK 5). Spatial entities, then, are to be conceived as complexes of relations or possible relations between things. Whitehead recognized that the adoption of the relational theory of space requires an investigation into the foundations of geometry.

> It [this investigation] has to describe what a point is, and has to show how the geometric relations between points issue from the ultimate relation between the ultimate things which are the immediate objects of knowledge (PNK 5).

13

We have just seen that Whitehead understands these "ultimate things which are the immediate objects of knowledge" to be (spatially and temporally extended) events. The ultimate relation is taken by Whitehead to be that of extension—a part-whole relationship of events. Thus Whitehead was concerned to derive geometrical entities from the fundamental concepts of extension and events. The method of derivation is that of extensive abstraction.

Before attempting a discussion of the method of extensive abstraction as systematically treated in PNK and CN, it will be convenient to consider one of Whitehead's early discussions of this method in order to see more clearly why Whitehead attempted to define geometrical entities by its application. The discussion of points in "The Anatomy of Some Scientific Ideas" is especially helpful (OT 162f). In this essay, Whitehead maintains the formation of the concept of points to depend upon a law called the "law of convergence to simplicity by diminution of extent" or, more simply, the "principle of convergence." This law states that the relations between or the aspects of sense presentation contained within two parts of two events are in an important respect more simple than the relations between the whole events (OT 147). Whitehead maintains that "the origin of points is the effort to take full advantage of the principle of convergence to simplicity" (OT 162). Whitehead recognized the modern definition of a point as "an ideal limit by indefinitely continuing the process of diminishing a volume (or area)" to take account of the principle of convergence in some respects (OT 163). However, a point so defined is often referred to as a "convenient fiction." The description is in itself full of difficulties, and the nature of the difficulties it involves suggested to Whitehead precisely how the application of the principle of convergence in the formation of the concept of a point should be conceived.

With respect to the description of points as "convenient fictions," Whitehead remarks that whereas "fiction" implies a concept which does not correspond to any fact, the addition of the term "convenient" implies a concept which corresponds to some important facts. Whitehead raises the question as to what these facts could be conceived to be and maintains that the description of a point as an "ideal limit," if "ideal limit" is given the precise meaning it receives in the theory of series and of values of functions, is not helpful in determining an answer.

14

Thus, again, we are confronted with the question: What are the precise properties meant when a point is described as an ideal limit? The discussion which
now follows is an attempt to express the concept of a point in terms of thought-
objects of perception related together by the whole-and-part relation, considered
either as a time-relation or as a space-relation. If it is so preferred, it may be
considered that the discussion is directed towards a precise elucidation of the
term 'ideal limit' as often used in this connection (OT 164).

In the elucidation of the concept of a point as an "ideal limit" Whitehead rejects the view that a point is to be considered as an infinitesimal
region.[1] In this rejection the issue as to what are the properties to which
points correspond when they are thought as "convenient fictions" is
decisive. If points are "convenient fictions," they must, in some sense
correspond to factors given in sense-awareness. Infinitesimal regions
are not given in sense-awareness; only finite spatial regions are revealed
in sense-awareness. Hence it is to finite spatial regions that Whitehead
turns in order to arrive at an understanding of a point. In particular
Whitehead attempts to define a point (and elucidate the notion of an
"ideal limit") by the conception of a class or series of finite spatial
regions.

The mature theory of the method of extensive abstraction starts from
the concept of events as the field of the binary relation of extension. The
relation of extension is conceived, as we have seen, as a part-whole relationship. If we symbolize this relationship of "extending over" by the
capital letter K and the events which compose the field of K by the
lowercase letters a, b, c,. . ., we may summarize the fundamental properties of extension as follows: (1) If aKb, b is a proper part of a, or, what
is to say the same thing, a is a whole of which b is a proper part. (2) Any
two events a, b may stand in one of the following relations: Either aKb;
bKa, aKc and bKc but not aKb or bKa; or a and b are disjoint. The
axioms for the relation of extension differ slightly in PNK and CN; we
will state the list of CN and its symbolic equivalent. (1) Extension is a
transitive relation. (If aKb and bKc, then aKc.) (2) Every event contains
other events and (3) is contained in other events. (If aKc, there are
events such as b where aKb and bKc.)[2] (4) For any two finite events,
there are other events in which they are contained. (For any two events
a, b, there are events such as e which eKa and eKb.) (5) A special relation of junction can be maintained between two events a, b if there is
a third event c such that no part of c is separated from both a and b.

Then *a* and *b* constitute one event which can be thought of as their sum.

Having made clear how the relation of extension is to be conceived, Whitehead proceeds to define an abstractive class of events. Whitehead recognizes an abstractive class of events to be any class of events which possesses the following two properties: (1) for any two members of the class, one extends over or contains the other as a part, and (2) there is no event which is extended over or contained as a common part of every member of the class (CN 79). These properties assure that an abstractive class contains an infinite number of members.

The derivation of geometrical entities by the method of extensive abstraction depends in some sense upon the "properties of convergence" of abstractive classes as defined above. An illustration will be helpful at this point. In PNK Whitehead gives examples of abstractive classes which appear to converge to a point and a line respectively.

Consider a series of squares, concentric and similarly situated. Let the lengths of the sides of the successive squares, stated in order of diminishing size, be

$$h_1, h_2, \ldots h_n, \ldots.$$

Then each square extends over all the subsequent squares of the set. Also let

$$L_{n \to \infty} h_n = 0;$$

namely, let h_n tend to zero as n increases indefinitely. Then the set forms an abstractive class.

Again, consider a series of rectangles, concentric and similarly situated. Let the lengths of the sides of the successive rectangles, stated in order of diminishing size, be $(a, h_1), (a, h_2), \ldots (a, h_n), \ldots$.

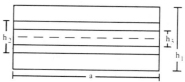

Thus one pair of opposite sides is of the same length throughout the whole series. Then each rectangle extends over all the subsequent rectangles. Let h_n tend to zero as n increases indefinitely. Then the set forms an abstractive class.

Evidently the set of squares converges to a point, and the set of rectangles to a straight line. Similarly, using three dimensions and volumes, we can thus diagrammatically find abstractive classes which converge to areas . . . (PNK 105-106n).

These spatial diagrams, although helpful in understanding White-head's meaning of an abstractive class, are, at the same time, misleading. We have just referred to the fact that the defining conditions of an abstractive class guarantee that the class contains an infinite number of members. The spatial diagrams, on the other hand, might suggest that the class has a terminus; in the diagrams considered, the termini appear to be the geometrical entities, point and straight line. However White-head's meaning is not that a point or a straight line is the smallest member of a particular abstractive class of events. Indeed Whitehead explicitly maintains that an abstractive class does not converge to a limiting event which is not a member of the class (CN 80). The fact that an abstractive class does not converge to a limiting event is of the utmost importance for the understanding of Whitehead's conception of geometrical entities, and we need to explore this thesis further.

In CN Whitehead develops the thesis that abstractive classes converge to no definite limit by the use of symbols. He defines s as the abstractive class of events $e_1, e_2, e_3, \ldots, e_n, e_{n+1}, \ldots$, where every e_i extends over the subsequent members e_{i+1}, e_{i+2}. Whitehead expresses the fact that the abstractive class s converges to nothing by the following symbolic expression: $s = e_1, e_2, e_3, \ldots, e_n, e_{n+1} \longrightarrow$ nothing. There is, however, a series associated with this abstractive class which can be said to converge to definite limits (CN 81). This class is defined as q (s) = q (e_1), q (e_2), q (e_3), $\ldots$, q (e_n), q (e_{n+1}), $\ldots$; q (s) is the class of quantitative expressions characterizing the internal and external relations of successive events. Although the series q (s) does not have a terminus, it can be said to converge to a class of limits. These limits depend upon quantitative measurements Q found in q (s). That is to say, if Q_1 is a quantitative measurement found in q (e_1) and Q_2 the homologue to Q_1 found in q (e_2), and so on, the series $Q_1, Q_2, Q_3, \ldots,$ $Q_n, Q_{n+1}, \ldots$ does converge to a definite limit. Then q (s) may be said to converge to a class of limits l (s) determined by homologous quantities found in the elements of q (s). Then, although the set s of abstractive events does not converge, there is a convergent series q (s) corresponding to s.

> Thus the set s does indicate an ideal simplicity of natural relations, though this simplicity is not the character of any actual event in s. We can make an approximation to such a simplicity which, as estimated numerically, is as close

17

as we like by considering an event which is far enough down the series towards the small end. It will be noted that it is the infinite series, as it stretches away in unending succession towards the small end, which is of importance. The arbitrarily large event with which the series starts has no importance at all. We can arbitrarily exclude any set of events at the big end of an abstractive set without the loss of any important property to the set as thus modified (CN 81-82).

Whitehead calls this "limiting character" or "ideal simplicity" of natural relations indicated by an abstractive set its "intrinsic character" and the properties in terms of which an abstractive set is defined its "extrinsic character." The significance of the principle of convergence for geometrical entities is, then, the "emergence of a definite intrinsic character from an abstractive set" (CN 82). This intrinsic character is determined by the extrinsic character of an abstractive set. "Accordingly there are different types of extrinsic character of convergence which lead to the approximation to different types of intrinsic characters as limits" (CN 83).

There are different connections possible between abstractive classes. Two such connections are important for our discussion—covering and equivalence. Whitehead understands one abstractive class A to cover another B when every member of A contains some members of B as its parts. When each of two abstractive classes A, B covers the other, A and B are said to be "equal in abstractive force" or, more simply, equivalent. The particular significance of equivalent abstractive classes lies in the fact that they converge to the same intrinsic character. Whitehead defines an abstractive element to be a complete class of equivalent abstractive classes. Geometrical entities are then defined to be abstractive elements. We may consider Whitehead's definition of a point of space as an abstractive element.

The first thing to do is to get hold of the class of abstractive elements which are in some sense the points of space. Such an abstractive element must in some sense exhibit a convergence to an absolute minimum of intrinsic character. Euclid has expressed for all time the general idea of a point, as being without parts and without magnitude. It is this character of being an absolute minimum which we want to get at and to express in terms of the extrinsic characters of the abstractive sets which make up a point. Furthermore, points which are thus arrived at represent the ideal of events without any extension, though there are in fact no such entities as these ideal events (CN 85-86).

Then points, lines, and areas are to be defined as emerging intrinsic characters of abstractive sets. On Whitehead's view, unlike the conception of a point as the "ideal limit" of convergent spatial regions, i.e., an infinitesimal region, points and other geometrical entities are not the same kind of entities as the converging spatial regions by which they are defined. Whitehead rules out this possibility by maintaining an abstractive class to have no limit. On Whitehead's view, there is no point (line, or area) independent of the classes of "converging" spatial regions; a point (line, or area) is identified with the classes of "converging" spatial regions. Hence geometrical entities are not properties of events; they merely represent an ideal to which members of an abstractive class approximate more and more closely as one goes farther and farther down the small end of the series. This ideal does not exist independently of the abstractive class. "But this ideal is in fact the ideal of a nonentity" (CN 61).

It seems that no definitive ontological implications for geometrical entities are entailed by their definition by the method of extensive abstraction. However one can point to definite tendencies for an ontological interpretation. Let us simplify the investigation by limiting our discussion to a consideration of implications for the ontological status of points. First, a point has no independent being; however it exists, it has dependent being. The concept of a point is formed by (1) recognizing a spatial region and (2) diminishing it as a series which contains no terminus. Since the series contains no terminus, the point cannot be conceived to have the same being as the members of the series—the point does not have the same being as spatial regions. That is to say, the point is not a feature of events. Rather the point is defined by the entire series of diminishing regions or, more precisely, by the class of all diminishing series of regions whose intrinsic character is an absolute minimum. On this conception, the point *is* the process or the "thought" activity of diminishing a region. This determination of the geometrical entity, *viz.,* the point, as the outcome of a mental activity suggests that a possible implication of the method of extensive abstraction for the ontological status of points is that there is no point apart from the activity of constructing it. In a very important respect a point is to be conceived as a product of thought.

On the other hand there is evidence against such a determination of points in Whitehead's first requirement in the conception of a point, *viz.,*

19

a finite spatial region *given* in sense-awareness. The definite connection made here between experience and the constructing of the geometrical entity can be interpreted as an implicit return to objectivism in the sense that if a definite connection is recognized between experience and the constructing, it is difficult to maintain that the resulting construction is a mere mental entity, i.e., that its being depends entirely upon the thought that thinks it.

Thus it seems that the method of extensive abstraction suggests both a tendency to a determination of geometrical entities as mental constructs and, at the same time, a tendency to an objectivist standpoint in some sense. These two aspects of Whitehead's conception of geometrical entities are not reconciled in the writings of the second period.

3. The thesis of the third period

The discussion of extensive abstraction in Whitehead's later and explicitly metaphysical work PR involves important modifications in this method. For the purposes of our discussion we need not consider in any detail the systematic difficulties involved in Whitehead's earlier definition of points which brought about the modifications in PR. A brief statement of the nature of these difficulties, however, will be helpful. Problems arose in connection with the part-whole relation of extension used in the derivation of spatial concepts. In brief, the difficulty was that the definition of points by means of this relation placed so great an emphasis on temporal extendedness that critics claimed that the derivation of spatial entities by this relation was not, as Whitehead had maintained, dependent on direct experience but, rather, contradicted it.[3] The modification of the method of extensive abstraction in PR takes account of these criticisms by starting from a different relation, "extensive connection," of which the relata are "regions" rather than events. This modification allowed the general method of extensive abstraction to be developed before the introduction of the distinction between space and time.

The systematic treatment of the method of extensive abstraction in PR starts from the fundamental relation of extensive connection. White-

20

head illustrates the relation of extensive connection between two regions by a set of diagrams. These diagrams indicate that two regions are extensively connected when they partially or wholly overlap or when they have contact at a single point or along parts of their boundaries. Whitehead sets out the basic properties of this relation of extensive connection, or more simply connection, by means of definitions and assumptions. He first defines two regions as "mediately connected" to mean that they are both connected with a third region. The assumptions include the following: (1) the relation of connection is symmetrical but not transitive, (2) no region is connected with all other regions, (3) any two regions are mediately connected, and (4) no region is connected or mediately connected with itself. The second definition states what is to be understood by the inclusion of one region in another: One region A includes another B when every region connected with B is also connected with A. Whitehead then sets out further assumptions which apply to all regions; we need not consider these for the purposes of our discussion.

The concept of an abstractive class, which is necessary for the definition of geometrical entities, depends upon a particular kind of inclusion which Whitehead calls "nontangential" inclusion. This type of inclusion is, perhaps, most clearly understood when compared with other types of inclusion. Whitehead distinguishes the following. (1) Two regions A, B "overlap" when there is a third region included in both A and B.[4] (2) Two regions A, B are "externally connected" when they are connected but do not overlap.[5] (3) Region B is "tangentially included" in region A when both B is included in A, and there are regions externally connected with both A and B.[6] (4) Region B is "nontangentially included" in region A when both B is included in A, and there is no third region externally connected with both A and B.[7] Whitehead then defines an abstractive class in terms of non-tangential inclusion.

> A set of regions is called an 'abstractive set,' when (i) any two members of the set are such that one of them includes the other non-tangentially, (ii) there is no region included in every member of the set (PR 454).

The relations of covering and equivalence necessary for the definition of geometrical entities depend upon the relation of inclusion with respect to abstractive classes. One abstractive class a includes another β when every member of a includes some members of β. Whitehead's

21

summary is strikingly similar to the accounts in his earlier writings.

> It is to be noticed that each abstractive set is to be conceived with its members in serial order, determined by the relation of inclusion. The series starts with a region of any size, and converges indefinitely towards smaller and smaller regions, without any limiting region. When the set a covers the set β, each member of a includes all the members of the convergent tail of β. Provided that we start far enough down in the serial arrangement of the set β, it will be found that though an abstractive set must start with *some* region at its big end, these initial large-sized regions never enter into our reasoning. Attention is always fixed on what relations occur when we have proceeded *far enough down* the series. The only relations which are interesting are those which, if they commence anywhere, continue throughout the remainder of the infinite series (PR 455).

Two abstractive classes are defined to be equivalent when each class covers the other. As in the earlier theory a complete group of abstractive classes, equivalent to each other but not equivalent to any abstractive class outside the group, is an abstractive, or geometrical, element. Points and line segments are defined in terms of such geometrical elements. The definition of a point requires the notion of "incidence." Of two nonidentical geometrical elements a and b, a is incident in b when every member of b covers every member of a. A point is then defined as that geometrical element with no geometrical element incident in it (PR 456). The definition of a line segment requires the concept of being "prime in reference to assigned conditions," *viz.,* (1) every member of the geometrical element satisfies the assigned conditions, (2) if any abstractive class satisfies the assigned conditions, then every member of the geometrical element associated with it also satisfies them, (3) no geometrical element whose members satisfy the assigned conditions is also incident in the given geometrical element. A segment between two points P, Q is defined to be a geometrical element prime with respect to the condition that the points P and Q are incident in it (PR 457).[8]

We may now turn to the question as to what implications, if any, these modified definitions hold for the ontological status of points and line segments. It seems to me that, in spite of the modifications made in the method of extensive abstraction, geometrical entities still appear, in a very important respect, to be the product of a mental activity. That is to say, the method of extensive abstraction does not account for the existence of points and segments independently of the infinitely diminishing regions which define them. Whitehead still is maintaining that the diminishing series has no limiting region.

4. The implications of Whitehead's metaphysics for the ontological status of geometrical entities

The method of extensive abstraction, however, is not the only source of information we have available to us to assist us in the determination of the status of abstractions in Whitehead's thought. The metaphysical inquiry in PR and the "metaphysical chapters" of SMW (Chapters X and XI) contain definite implications for the status of abstractions which are contrary to the determination implied in the definition of geometrical entities by the method of extensive abstraction. The remainder of this section will be concerned with making explicit these implications.

In PR Whitehead states that he is in agreement with Aristotle as to the fundamental metaphysical task and thus accepts the principle that the entities which exist in the full sense are the only actual things. Whitehead terms this fundamental metaphysical principle the "ontological principle."

> . . . the general Aristotelian principle is maintained that, apart from things that are actual, there is nothing—nothing either in fact or in efficacy. . . . This general principle will be termed the 'ontological principle.' It is the principle that everything is positively somewhere in actuality. . .(PR 64).

Whitehead, then, is in agreement with Aristotle that the things which are actual are particular things. However Aristotle and Whitehead do not conceive the nature of the particular things which exist in the full sense of "to be" in the same way. Nonetheless Whitehead's doctrine of "actual entity" contains important implications for the ontological status of mathematical entities. We will approach these implications by an elucidation of Whitehead's conception of actual entity.[9]

The complete characterization of the nature of actual entities would involve the elaboration of Whitehead's entire metaphysical scheme. Such an undertaking is, of course, beyond the limits of this essay. Here we can merely provide a description of actual entities adequate for the understanding of the being of some of the other entities dependent upon them.

Whitehead conceives the fundamental feature of an actual entity to be process, agency, act. "The very essence of real actuality—that is, of the completely real—is *process.* Thus each actual thing is only to be understood in terms of its becoming and perishing" (AI 354). The actual world is a macroscopic process, and its process is constituted by the microscopic processes of actual entities. That is to say, the actual world is composed of *individual acts* or *unit* processes of activity. The process of an actual entity consists in becoming. Since the fundamental metaphysical feature of an actual entity by virtue of which it is an actuality is process and this process is becoming, the very being of an actual entity is its becoming (PR 33-35). This becoming terminates in a novel unity which Whitehead calls a concrescence. Whitehead maintains this concrescence to be a concrescence of antecedent actualities into a novel unity and to be constituted by an actual entity's taking a definite form. The latter notion requires considerable elucidation.

The ontological principle guarantees that actual entities are the only actual things. This does not mean, as we have seen, that no other kind of entity exists; rather the ontological principle requires that other kinds of entity "exist" only in a derivative sense, *viz.,* as "components" of or "abstractions" from actual entities.

> Thus the actual world is built up of actual occasions; and by the ontological principle whatever things there are in any sense of 'existence,' are derived by abstraction from actual occasions (PR 113).

The very concept of an actual entity, an individual act, entails the existence of entities of a kind different from actual entities. We have seen that for an actual entity to become—to terminate in a novel unity —it must take on a *definite form.* Hence another kind of entity, *viz.,* "form of definiteness," is implicated in creative activity.

> . . . the actualities constituting the process of the world are conceived as exemplifying the ingression (or 'participation') of other things which constitute the potentialities of definiteness for any actual existence. The things that are temporal arise by their participation in the things which are eternal (PR 63).

"Forms of definiteness" is another name for the entities Whitehead calls "eternal objects." Whitehead understands eternal objects to be Platonic Ideas. "These forms of definiteness are the Platonic forms, the Platonic ideas, the medieval universals" (FR 32).

Whitehead's choice of the term "eternal object" is in need of elaboration. We can perhaps best understand the meaning of *eternal* objects by contrasting their being with that of actual entities. We have already referred to the fact that the being of actual entities is constituted by their becoming. Actual entities come into existence; they are novel creations. The being of eternal objects, on the other hand, is not a process of becoming. "The eternal objects are the same for all actual entities" (PR 34). Eternal objects come into being only in the sense that they determine the definiteness of actual entities; eternal objects are not novel creations (PR 33). In calling these entities eternal *objects,* Whitehead is insisting that forms are not to be conceived as the outcome of a mental activity. Eternal objects must be "given" to actualities in becoming and are, thus, "objects" for these actualities.

The ontological principle requires that eternal objects exist only as components of actual entities. Whitehead understands eternal objects to exist as forms of definiteness of the things that are actual.

> That an eternal object can be described only in terms of its potentiality for 'ingression' into the becoming of actual entities; and that its analysis only discloses other eternal objects. It is a pure potential. The term 'ingression' refers to the particular mode in which the potentiality of an eternal object is realized in a particular actual entity, contributing to the definiteness of that actual entity (PR 34).

The passage just quoted refers to a second aspect of eternal objects. For Whitehead, eternal objects are not only the definiteness of particular actual entities. If they were so conceived, the *only* eternal objects would be those eternal objects which constitute the definiteness of actual entities. Thus there could be nothing in the universe which is not there at the present moment; it would, thus, not be possible for there to be any difference from what there is at the present moment. This would mean that possibility is an empty concept. For Whitehead, however, the concept of possibility is not at all empty. The universe is capable of being different than it now is; certain beings not actual now possibly will be. That is to say, entities could have a definiteness different from the definiteness they now have. Then an eternal object could not be only the definiteness of particular actual entities.

We must recognize another aspect of eternal objects, *viz.,* their universal aspect—eternal objects may be considered *in abstraction from* their ingression into actual entities. So considered, eternal objects are *pure potentials.* They are *potentials for* the determination of definiteness of actualities.[10] Then, although eternal objects must exist as components of some actual entity, there is nothing in their nature which determines of which actual entity they will be a component.

> An eternal object is always a potentiality for actual entities; but in itself, as conceptually felt, it is neutral as to the fact of its physical ingression in any particular actual entity of the temporal world. 'Potentiality' is the correlative of 'givenness.' The meaning of 'givenness' is that what *is* 'given' might not have been 'given'; and that what *is not* 'given' might have been 'given' (PR 70).

Whitehead is maintaining that eternal objects are not reducible to actuality but, rather, constitute a distinct metaphysical feature of the universe. However Whitehead does not accept the Platonic position that eternal objects are themselves actualities. For Whitehead eternal objects have a metaphysical status distinct from actuality, although they cannot exist separate from actuality.[11] Then an eternal object transcends actuality in an important sense, and as transcendent, an eternal object must have an "intrinsic nature" of its own.

> Eternal objects are thus, in their nature, abstract. By 'abstract' I mean that what an eternal object is in itself—that is to say, its essence—is comprehensible without reference to some one particular occasion of experience. To be abstract is to transcend particular concrete occasions of actual happening. But to transcend an actual occasion does not mean being disconnected from it. On the contrary, I hold that each eternal object has its proper connection with each other such occasion, which I term its mode of ingression into that occasion (SMW 228-29).

Two points are important in reference to this characterization of eternal objects. (1) Each eternal object "is what it is"; i.e., each eternal object has an individual essence by virtue of which it is this eternal object and not something else. As such, its status is that of "a possibility for actuality" (SMW 229). The actuality is a selection among these possibilities, and this selection involves a gradation of possibilities with respect to their actualization in the occasion. This consideration leads us to the second point. (2) Each eternal object, as a possibility for actuality, is inseparable from its reference to other eternal objects and to actuality generally. Whitehead expresses this aspect of an eternal object by saying it has a "relational essence" (SMW 230). Let us first consider this relational essence of an eternal object in regard to other eternal objects.

To say that an eternal object has a relational essence means that an eternal object stands in a determinate relatedness to every other eternal object. Further, these relations are constitutive of an eternal object; they determine what the eternal object is. Then an inherent structural relatedness belongs to the nature of eternal objects. This basic fact of togetherness of all eternal objects leads Whitehead to describe eternal objects in their intrinsic interrelatedness as a "realm."

> The determinate relatedness of the eternal object A to every other eternal object is how A is systematically and by the necessity of its nature related to every other eternal object. Such relatedness represents a possibility for realization. But a relationship is a fact which concerns all the implicated relata, and cannot be isolated as if involving only one of the relata. Accordingly there is a general fact of systematic mutual relatedness which is inherent in the character of possibility. The realm of eternal objects is properly described as a 'realm,' because each eternal object has its status in this general systematic complex of mutual relatedness (SMW 231).

An investigation of the nature of eternal objects as abstractions, then, reveals that eternal objects stand in a "general systematic complex of mutual relatedness." This aspect of eternal objects as the possible interrelatedness of actuality is, it seems to me, that which Whitehead conceived the science of mathematics to study. There is evidence for this interpretation in Whitehead's discussion of "Science and Philosophy" in AI. There Whitehead writes:

> The general science of mathematics is concerned with the investigation of patterns of connectedness, in abstraction from the particular relata and the particular modes of connection. It is only in some special branches of mathematics that notions of quantity and number are dominant themes. The real point is that the essential connectedness of things can never be safely omitted (AI 197).

If the mathematical is to be conceived as this "general systematic complex of mutual relatedness," we need now to determine precisely how eternal objects and, in particular, eternal objects as pure potentials, exist. The ontological principle allows us to identify this question with that of the relation of eternal objects to actuality.

The "relational essence" of an eternal object with respect to actuality means that an eternal object must have a capacity, or indeterminateness, for relations to actual entities. The relationships of a particular eternal object to an actual entity are simply how its eternal relationships to all other eternal objects are graded in respect to their realization in the actual entity. Although there is an indeterminateness on the side of a particular eternal object with respect to its ingression into a particular actual entity, there is a determinateness as regards the actual entity as to the ingression of the eternal object. The selection of an eternal object for actualization, then, includes the synthetic prehension of all eternal objects and, thus, involves the whole pattern of interconnectedness exhibited by eternal objects. Every actualization involves the whole realm of eternal objects.

> It has already been emphasized that an actual occasion is to be conceived as a limitation; and that this process of limitation can be still further characterized as a gradation. This characteristic of an actual occasion (*a*, say) requires further elucidation: An indeterminateness stands in the essence of any eternal object (*A*, say). The actual occasion *a* synthesises in itself every eternal object; and, in so doing, it includes the *complete* determinate relatedness of *A* to every other eternal object, or set of eternal objects. This synthesis is a limitation of realization but *not* of content. Each relationship preserves its inherent self-identity (SMW 233).

We see, then, that an eternal object "exists" by virtue of being realized in an actual entity and that this realization involves the whole pattern of interconnectedness displayed by eternal objects. However this aspect of the "existence" of an eternal object does not exhaust the relation of eternal objects to actuality. In particular we must raise the question as to the "existence" of eternal objects considered in their aspect as pure potentials. In this aspect we have seen that eternal objects are essentially interrelated. What can be the relation of this "realm" of eternal objects to actuality; i.e., the relation of eternal objects to actuality when they are not realized in actual entities? The question is not nonsensical, for Whitehead is insistent that even in their transcendent aspect, eternal objects must be "relevant" to actuality. This is Whitehead's meaning when he maintains that eternal objects must be "somewhere."

> Everything must be somewhere; and here 'somewhere' means 'some actual entity.' Accordingly the general potentiality of the universe must be somewhere; since it retains its proximate relevance to actual entities for which it is unrealized (PR 73).

That is to say, the ontological principle requires that the "general systematic complex of mutual relatedness" of eternal objects must itself be referred to some actuality. Just as we cannot understand the "existence" of a particular eternal object apart from its reference to an actual entity, we cannot understand the being of this "realm" apart from some actuality. For the reasons given above, the existence of such a realm cannot be referred to any "temporal" actual entity. Like many antecedent thinkers, Whitehead refers the being of eternal objects in their transcendent aspect to the mind of God.

> This 'proximate relevance' reappears in subsequent concrescence as final causation regulative of the emergence of novelty. This 'somewhere' is the non-temporal actual entity. Thus, 'proximate relevance' means 'relevance as in the primordial mind of God' (PR 73).

God does not create the eternal objects; rather his relation to the eternal objects is to be conceived as a "conceptual valuation" of the multiplicity of eternal objects.

> He does not create eternal objects; for his nature requires them in the same degree that they require him. This is an exemplification of the coherence of the categoreal types of existence. The general relationships of eternal objects to each other, relationships of diversity and of pattern, are their relationships in God's conceptual realization. Apart from this realization, there is mere isolation indistinguishable from nonentity (PR 392).

Eternal objects, then, are conceived to "exist" in two ways—as the definiteness of actual entities and, in their aspect of transcending any particular instance of ingression, as a conceptual realization in the mind of God.

In a passage from AI quoted above we saw that the general science of mathematics studies patterns of connectedness, considered in abstraction from the particular relata and modes of connection, and that the notions of number, quantity, particular geometrical relations, etc., come into question only in the special branches of mathematics. In order to understand these more special mathematical entities, we need to consider Whitehead's classification of eternal objects.

Whitehead classifies eternal objects on the basis of the way in which they ingress into actual entities.

> An eternal object can only function in the concrescence of an actual entity in one of three ways: (i) it can be an element in the definiteness of some objectified nexus, or of some single actual entity, which is the datum of a feeling; (ii) it can be an element in the definiteness of the subjective form of some feeling; or

29

(iii) it can be an element in the datum of a conceptual, or propositional, feeling. All other modes of ingression arise from integrations which presuppose these modes (PR 445).

Whitehead understands the third mode to be a "restricted ingression" in the sense that it involves only the conceptual valuation of a possible ingression in the first or second mode. The first two modes, on the other hand, are the modes in which the ingression of an eternal object is "unrestrictedly realized." This does not mean, however, that every eternal object can ingress in both of these modes. Whitehead maintains that some eternal objects can obtain ingression only in the first mode. This fact is the basis of the classification of eternal objects into members of the "objective" and "subjective" species. Eternal objects of the objective species function in the concrescence of an actual entity as an element in the definiteness of an actual entity or nexus.[12] This is to say that an eternal object of the objective species functions only *relationally:* "By a necessity of its nature it is introducing one actual entity, or nexus, into the real internal constitution of another actual entity" (PR 445). Whitehead maintains the eternal objects of this species to be mathematical Platonic Forms.

> A member of this species inevitably introduces into the immediate subject other actualities. The definiteness with which it invests the external world may, or may not, conform to the real internal constitutions of the actualities objectified. But conformably, or non-conformably, such is the character of that nexus for that actual entity. This is a real physical fact, with its physical consequences. Eternal objects of the objective species are the mathematical platonic forms (PR 446).

A mathematical form, then, serves to relate actual entities; more precisely, it serves to introduce "one actual entity, or nexus, into the real internal constitution of another actual entity." It is important to see that this relation is constituted by an actualization of form. That is to say, the actual entities are really related by virtue of their actualization of a form in common. When actual entities realize a form in common, they exhibit a pattern, a character, a structure. This pattern, character, or structure, considered in abstraction from its actualization by actual entities, is an eternal object in its aspect of pure potentiality. Whitehead conceives the mathematical forms to be abstractions from all qualitative features of such pattern, character, or structure. "The extremity of abstraction from all qualitative elements reduces pattern to a bare mathematical form" (AI 326).

It remains now to make explicit the implications of these metaphysical considerations for particular geometrical entities such as points and line segments.

Whitehead conceived geometry to be the theory of extensive connection, or extension, and in his late writings he conceived extension to be the most general form of relationship between actual entities (PR 441). This conception of extension is contrary to the position of the earlier works, PNK and CN, in which Whitehead first put forward the systematic theory of extensive abstraction. There, we have seen, Whitehead conceived extension to be a feature of events, hence of actuality. In PR Whitehead is rejecting this earlier conception of extension—extension is a relation; its characteristics are derived not from actuality, but from form. As a form, extension is a possibility for actuality. Extension is the most general complex of possible relatedness; it is the most general structure exhibited in common by actual entities. Whitehead, then, understands extensiveness to be the scheme of *potential* standpoints and, as such, extensiveness constitutes a continuum. Whitehead describes this extensive continuum as "the general system of relatedness of all possibilities, in so far as the system is limited by its relevance to the general fact of actuality" (SMW 233). "All actual entities are related according to the determinations of this continuum" (PR 103).

Whitehead's theory is that the continuum is to be conceived as the mere potentiality for division; actual entities atomize the continuum (PR 104). Then at any standpoint there is a possibility for division of the continuum into other actual entities defining the universe from their particular standpoints. This is to say that the standpoint of an actual entity involves a geometrical relation with respect to all other standpoints. Thus there are geometrical relations essential to the essence of the actual entities considered as potentials for division. "The 'extensive' scheme is nothing else than the generic morphology of the internal relations which bind the actual occasions into a nexus" (PR 441).

Actual entities, therefore, must stand in extensive relationships. When actual entities exhibit a pattern by virtue of their realization of a common form, one can abstract from the pattern to consider it solely in respect of the extensive relations it involves. Ordinary geometrical concepts are to be found among these extensive relationships; they are

forms of relationships between actual entities. I take this to be Whitehead's meaning when he writes: "Extension is a form of relationship between the actualities of a nexus. A point is a nexus of actual entities
with a certain 'form'; and so is a 'segment.' Thus geometry is the investigation of the morphology of nexūs" (PR 461).

Hence we see that the implications of Whitehead's metaphysics for
the status of geometrical entities are contrary to the conception of these
entities as the outcome of a mental activity. Rather, geometrical entities
are forms, eternal objects, which function relationally; they introduce
an actual entity into the real internal constitution of another actual entity or actual entities. Considered apart from their actualization by actual
entities, i.e., considered in their aspect of pure possibility for relatedness,
mathematical eternal objects have a definite status in the general pattern of interrelatedness which is ultimately referred to the mind of God.

Thus geometrical entities are not dependent for their being upon the
activity of the human mind as the theory of extensive abstraction might
suggest. Rather they are to be conceived as discoveries in the proper
sense. In order to see more clearly in what sense they are discovered, we
need to consider Whitehead's category of conceptual prehension.

Whitehead distinguishes physical and conceptual prehension. The
simplest case of a physical prehension is the prehension of òne actual
entity by another. A conceptual prehension differs from a physical prehension with respect to the datum of the prehension (PR 39-40). In
the simplest physical prehension the datum is an actual entity; in a conceptual prehension the datum is an eternal objèct. Further, the datum of
a conceptual prehension is an eternal object in its aspect of pure potentiality—in its general capacity for determination rather than as a realized
determinant of actuality. "A conceptual feeling is the feeling of an eternal object in respect to its general capacity as a determinant of character,
including thereby its capacity of exclusiveness" (PR 367).

The initial prehensions of an actual entity are physical prehensions.
The eternal objects which determine the definiteness of actualities then
become the data for conceptual prehensions. But the conceptual prehension is of the eternal object in its general capacity for determination—
as a pure potentiality, a pure possibility. Thus in conceptual prehension
eternal objects are discovered, not merely as features of actuality but as
what they are. The intrinsic nature of eternal objects is discovered in

conceptual prehension; in conceptual prehension one has an encounter with eternal objects as pure possibilities.

In mathematical thinking, the paradigm instance of conceptual thinking, one is concerned only with possibles. In thinking mathematically, one is exploring the structural relations among eternal objects which are contained in the essential nature of eternal objects as pure possibilities. It is in this sense that the mathematical, which we have seen to be the "general systematic complex of mutual relatedness," is to be characterized as a discovery for Whitehead.

II. Number

5. The thesis of the first period

The discussion of the ontological status of geometrical entities in the preceding section will greatly simplify our consideration of the status of number. However we need briefly to consider Whitehead's early treatment of number, for the implications of this early theory stand in sharp contrast to the implications for the status of number which can be drawn from the metaphysical considerations we have just taken into account.

Whitehead's early theory of number is the theory of PM. In this work Whitehead and Russell were concerned to arrive (among other things) at a *definition* of number. The definitions of the numbers 0, 1, 2, etc., and of cardinal and ordinal numbers generally, start from the notion of a unit class. "A *unit* class is the class of terms identical with a given term, i.e. the class whose only member is the given term" (PM I 329). Or, in symbols, ιx means "the class of terms which are identical with x" or "the class whose only member is x" (PM I *51 340). Thus a unit class is to be understood as a class of the form ιx (for some x). The cardinal number 1 is then defined as the class of all unit classes, or the class of all classes of the form ιx for some x (PM I*52 347). The definition of 2 requires the notion of couples. There are two kinds of couples: (1) cardinal couples ($\iota x \cup \iota y$ where the order of x and y is irrelevant) and (2) ordinal couples ($\iota x \uparrow \iota y$ where there is an order as between x and y). The cardinal number 2 is defined to be the class of all couples of the form $\iota x \cup \iota y$ (where $x \neq y$) and the ordinal number 2 to be the class of all couples of the form $\iota x \uparrow \iota y$ (where $x \neq y$) (PM I *54 359). The cardinal number 0 is next introduced and defined to be the null class ($\iota \Lambda$) (PM I *55 366). In general a cardinal number is defined to be a class of all similar classes (PM I *73 453).

As in the case of the definition of geometrical entities by the theory of extensive abstraction, the definition of number by the theory of classes

34

apparently has no definitive ontological implications. However the same tendencies to an ontological determination which we found in the method of extensive abstraction seem to apply to number as defined by classes. On the one side the definition of number by the theory of classes seems to suggest a determination of number as a mental entity. Although the decision as to the existence of classes is left open in PM (I 24), much evidence is presented against the conception of the existence of such entities as classes apart from their construction by the human mind (PM I 72, 187-89, 225). Further, in the earlier MC Whitehead remarked that the grave doubt as to the possibility of the existence of classes led him to write this memoir in such a manner that the concepts presented do not depend upon any theory of classes (MC 18). In any case a class is, in a very important respect, the outcome of a mental activity. The definition of cardinal numbers as classes of all similar classes, then, places a great deal of emphasis on the nature of number as a mere construct. On the other side it is clear that the treatment of number in PM presupposes a definite connection between the formation of classes and experience. Whitehead later recognized this connection to lead to many difficulties (ICNV). Whitehead came to maintain that the extensional definition of cardinal numbers in PM made number depend upon the metaphysical concept of types and the "shifting accidents of factual existence" (ICNV 321). This is to say that the meaning of each cardinal number is changed by changes in the number of countable objects.

> In short, according to the 'Principia' definition, arithmetic is bound up with intension and with history. According to that definition a new litter of pigs alters the meaning of every number, and of every extension of number, employed in mathematics (ICNV 321).

The attempt Whitehead made to overcome these difficulties and to arrive at a definition of number in purely logical terms need not concern us. We wish only to point out that Whitehead's early treatment of number involves a definite connection between number and experience.

6. The implications of Whitehead's metaphysics for the ontological status of number

Whitehead's later metaphysical discussions contain definite implications for the ontological status of number. We have already seen that Whitehead locates the mathematical forms among eternal objects of the objective species. Thus numbers, as well as geometrical relations, belong to the realm of eternal objects. Further, the understanding of Whitehead's conception of number depends in a special way upon grasping the relevance of forms to process. We have referred to the fact that Whitehead maintains that in so far as there is definiteness, there must be a form. Whitehead recognized that this thesis involves the further thesis that forms cannot be limited to static forms. In particular there must be forms of process. For Whitehead numbers are conceived to belong to this group of forms. The relevance of forms to process has important implications for the understanding of the nature of arithmetical truths. We will consider these implications as they are put forward in Whitehead's late work MT.

One of the most widely accepted interpretations of the nature of arithmetical truths at the time of the writing of MT as well as at present is that they are tautologies. Whitehead explicitly rejects this interpretation. His discussion centers around the example of "twice-three is six" (MT 123f). To understand this arithmetical law as a tautology is to understand "twice-three" to "say the same thing" as "six." That is, the law expresses no new truth. In Whitehead's view, however, these laws are not tautologies but have to do with a process and its issue. In particular, "twice-three." in the example refers to a form of process, and "six" is a characterization of the complex entity which issues from the process.

Whitehead illustrates his meaning by the consideration of the fusion into a single group of two groups, each of which is characterized by triplicity. The special form of this process of fusion is "twice-three." This form derives its character from the triplicity of each group, and the triplicity arises from some principle of individuation by virtue of which the group is said to display threeness. When the two groups fuse into one, the resultant group can be characterized in terms of number.

However the complex entity which is the issue of the fusion is not necessarily a group of six. Indeed it is a group of six only if the same principle of individuation involved in the original groups is preserved. If the principle of individuation is disturbed, the process will not issue into an entity characterized by the number six. Whitehead gives the example of the fusion of two groups of water beads, each group consisting of three beads. The issue of this fusion may be one bead or, if shattering occurs, perhaps fifty or more beads. The arithmetical law "twice-three is six," then, presupposes the preservation of this relevant principle of individuation. Such a principle of individuation is a rather vague notion. Nevertheless Whitehead maintains we are still able to understand what is meant by the concept of "twice-three" as referring to a form of process of fusion sustaining a relevant principle of individuation and of "six" as characterizing the complex entity into which the process issues. "The statement 'twice-three is six' is referent to an unspecified principle of sustenance of character which is supposed to be maintained during the process of fusion" (MT 125).

Numbers, then, are forms of process. Whitehead puts it:

> The very notion of number refers to the process from the individual units to the compound group. The final number belongs to no one of the units; it characterizes the way in which the group unity has been attained. Thus even the statement 'six equals six' need not be construed as a mere tautology. It can be taken to mean that six as dominating a special form of combination issues in six as a character of a datum for further process. There is no such entity as a mere static number. There are only numbers playing their parts in various processes conceived in abstraction from the world-process (MT 127-128).

Whitehead, then, determines number to characterize the way multiplicity is embraced into a unity. The way multiplicity is comprehended in a unity is, in Whitehead's view, not referred to mind, human or divine, but rather to form, to eternal objects.

We may conclude that for Whitehead the general science of pure mathematics studies the inherent structure of relatedness belonging to eternal objects as pure possibilities. Particular branches of mathematics have as their subject matter special mathematical forms which are initially patterns displayed by actual entities in relation and are abstracted by the mind. One arrives at geometrical forms by abstracting from a group of actual entities to consider only the extensive relationships

37

involved and at arithmetical forms by abstracting further still to consider the group only in respect to the way in which its unity has been attained. But in abstracting the forms constituting the definiteness of actualities, one does not, in Whitehead's view, attain the mathematical. For Whitehead the mathematical is attained only in a conceptual prehension, only when these abstracted forms are considered, not as the determinations of the definiteness of actualities but in their general capacity for determination, i.e., as pure possibilities. For Whitehead mathematical thinking is an exploration, and a discovery, of the structural relations among eternal objects as pure possibilities.

Part Two

FOUNDATIONAL CONCEPTS FOR THE PHILOSOPHY OF ORGANISM

III. Organism
and Environment

7. Organic mechanism

In his early development of a philosophy of organism, Whitehead uses the notion of "organic mechanism" as a replacement for "materialistic mechanism."

> I would term the doctrine of these lectures, the theory of *organic mechanism*. In this theory, the molecules may blindly run in accordance with the general laws, but the molecules differ in their intrinsic characters according to the general organic plans of the situations in which they find themselves (SMW 116).

> An individual entity, whose own life history is a part within the life-history of some larger, deeper, more complete pattern, is liable to have aspects of that larger pattern dominating its own being, and to experience modifications of that larger pattern reflected in itself as modifications of its own being. This is the theory of organic mechanism (SMW 156).

These are the only two passages in which the term "organic mechanism" occurs in SMW, and the term does not appear at all in subsequent works. Whitehead gives no explanation for dropping the term, but it would seem that a primary reason might be that the term "mechanism" remained so closely associated with materialism in both ordinary language and technical scientific and philosophical literature that "organic mechanism" suggested, at first glance, a contradiction in terms. However, a brief analysis of how Whitehead saw the compatibility of these terms is illuminating for setting out the basic metaphysical categories needed for the understanding of science.

"Organic" suggests the important doctrine of modification of parts in forming a whole, or, more precisely, of the modification of parts in wholes according to the plan of the whole. Whitehead repeatedly refers to such modification in SMW.

> The parts of the body are really portions of the environment of the total bodily event, but so related that their mutual aspects, each in the other, are peculiarly

effective in modifying the pattern of either. This arises from the intimate character of the relation of whole to part. The body is a portion of the environment for the part, and the part is a portion of the environment for the body; only they are peculiarly sensitive, each to the modification of the other. This sensitiveness is so arranged that the part adjusts itself to preserve the stability of the pattern of the body (SMW 214).

The concrete enduring entities are organisms, so that the plan of the *whole* influences the very characters of the subordinate organisms which enter into it. In the case of an animal, the mental states enter into the plan of the total organism and thus modify the plans of the successive subordinate organisms until the ultimate smallest organisms, such as electrons, are reached. Thus an electron within a living body is different from an electron outside it, by reason of the plan of the body. The electron blindly runs either within or without the body; but it runs within the body in accordance with its character within the body; that is to say, in accordance with the general plan of the body, and this plan includes the mental state. But the principle of modification is perfectly general throughout nature, and represents no property peculiar to living bodies (SMW 115-16).

"Mechanism" suggests the complete disassociation of Whitehead's doctrine from that of vitalism and of the dualism which vitalism accepts (SMW 150). At the same time "mechanism" affirms the essential law-likeness of all nature, including the law-likeness of modification. That is, the behavior of any part in any whole can be given an explanation, but the explanation may differ according to the situation in which the parts are found. However their behavior in similar situations can be expected to be accounted for by the same, or at least analogous, explanations.

It seems possible that there may be physical laws expressing the modification of the ultimate basic organisms when they form part of higher organisms with adequate compactness of pattern. It would, however, be entirely in consonance with the empirically observed actions of environments, if the direct effects of aspects as between the whole body and its parts were negligible. We should expect transmission. In this way the modification of total pattern would transmit itself by means of a series of modifications of a descending series of parts, so that finally the modification of the cell changes its aspect in the molecule, thus effecting a corresponding alteration in the molecule—or in some subtler entity. Thus the question for physiology is the question of the physics of molecules in cells of different characters (SMW 215-16).

It seems, then, that "organic mechanism" may be interpreted as involving certain theses with respect to the relationship between wholes and parts.

First, in wholes where modification occurs, properties of higher levels of organization cannot be deduced from properties of lower levels of organization when the premises consist merely of statements about the parts in that relationship. What must be added are premises elaborating a theory which describes the behavior of those parts in forming wholes. That is, only from theoretical statements describing, generally, the potentiality of parts to organize wholes and the statement of the condition of a particular organizing relation can a statement describing a whole with particular properties be deduced. Hence wholes in which modification occurs are not aggregates. In aggregates, theories about the parts (taken individually) suffice to deduce their relationship in wholes. In wholes involving modification, wider theories are required for the deduction; these theories affirm the potentiality of parts to behave differently in and out of the various wholes they can organize.

Second, understanding of wholes involving modification can be gained by an understanding of the parts only when there is a theory explaining the relations of the parts in wholes. Such understanding is possible because the theory involves statements about the potential relationships of parts in the various wholes they organize. Then the behavior of a part in a given whole can be deduced from its full range of possible behaviors.

Third, there is a reciprocity in the determination of parts and whole; the parts determine the whole in the sense that the whole is an organization of the parts (the parts in interrelationship), but there is modification of parts according to the wholes they organize and thereby determination of the parts by the whole.

These theses are essentially an affirmation of the internal relatedness of part and whole for some complexes, *viz.,* wholes involving modification. If parts have potential to act differently in different wholes, parts are modified according to the wholes they organize, and a complete description of parts involves reference to this modification, then the interrelationship of parts is not distinguishable from the nature of parts. In parts, the possibilities for relationship are constitutive of their nature.

8. Organism

In discussing the reciprocity of part and whole Whitehead used the suggestive terms "organism" and "environment." ("The body [whole] is a portion of the environment for the part, and the part is a portion of the environment for the body"; "The concrete enduring entities are organisms, so that the plah of the *whole* influences the very characters of the subordinate organisms which enter into it.") His usage here is clearly a stretching of the ordinary usage of these terms. I wish to suggest that an elucidation of these stretched meanings provides a framework for the discussion of the fundamental issues in the philosophy of science.

The biological meaning of the term "organism" is (1) "a living being" (as opposed to lifeless matter) and (2) "a totality whose various parts or elements are related to each other according to some principle which is derived from the whole itself. . . . A system."[1]

Whitehead clearly understands "organism" to involve both of these meanings. However a consideration of discussions of life in his late works makes it clear that "a living being" is not to be taken as the generic meaning.

Whitehead maintained that SMW, PR, and AI are to be considered as supplementary of each other in the development of the philosophy of organism (AI Preface). The discussions of what it means to be living differ in PR and AI from the meaning of "organism" first put forward in SMW.

In PR Whitehead gives three criteria for marking off living from non-living organisms. First, living organisms exhibit novelty in response to stimuli (PR 155). These novel responses are made possible by a conceptual initiative; that is, these "reactions are inexplicable by *any* tradition of pure physical inheritance" (PR 159). As in the case of all conceptual initiative, Whitehead is maintaining that underlying the novel responses are goals—diverse and alternative goals (PR 159). This criterion is meant to make a distinction between higher and lower living organisms and between living organisms and nonliving complexes, which is a distinction in degree and not in kind (PR 156). Second, living organisms are sustained by nonliving complexes. There is a protection of living organisms by inorganic complexes; yet there is a reciprocity: Nonliving

44

systems provide an environment for a living organism, but the responses of the living organisms are protective of the whole system (PR 157). Third, living organisms require food. Hence to be alive is in some sense to be a robber of the non-living environment (PR 160).

In AI Whitehead emphasizes the first-mentioned criterion of PR. "The essence of life is the teleological introduction of novelty, with some conformation of objectives" (AI 266). Here the meaning of this criterion is significantly clarified: "Life is the coordination of the mental spontaneeities throughout the occasions of a society" (AI 266). Life is characterized by a coordination of conceptual initiative towards a goal which, although present in nonliving complexes, is averaged out by the lack of coordination.[2]

The discussions of "life" and "living" in PR and AI point to the highly specific nature of living organisms. In SMW, where the centrality of the concept of organism first emerges, "organism" is used in a sense more general than "living organism." Here Whitehead used the term "organism" to refer to physical as well as biological entities.

> Science is taking on a new aspect which is neither purely physical nor purely biological. It is becoming the study of organisms. Biology is the study of larger organisms; whereas physics is the study of the smaller organisms (SMW 150).
>
> There are not only basic organisms [those incapable of further analysis]. . . . There are also organisms of organisms. Suppose for the moment and for the sake of simplicity, we assume, without any evidence, that electrons and hydrogen nuclei are such basic organisms. Then the atoms, and the molecules, are organisms of a higher type, which also represent a compact definite organic unity (SMW 161).

These passages suggest that "life" is not the generic sense of organism. Rather the primary reference of this term is to complexes in which there is a modification of parts according to a "principle derived from the whole itself." This constitutes a rejection of organisms as materialistic machines. In this interpretation "organism" can refer to atoms, molecules, even ecosystems, for in each case there is modification of the parts in accordance with the pattern of the more complex hierarchically structured whole. In what follows "organism" will be taken in this general sense of organic unity. "A living being" is a very special kind of organism.

9. Environment

"Organisms" and "environment" are correlatives. Hence the understanding of "environment" cannot be separated from that of "organism."

"Environment" is not one of the explicitly set out categories of Whitehead's metaphysical scheme, and no discussion of its meaning is to be found in his writings. Whitehead's use of the term is equivocal. I shall attempt to argue that his use of "environment" is not sheerly equivocal, but, rather, equivocal by reference to a generic sense. It is the purpose of this section to come to an understanding of this generic sense. In order to do so, it will be helpful to consider passages in which the term is used in different senses.

The uses Whitehead makes of the term cluster around three different senses:

(1) "environment" as (a) order expressed by organisms and (b) order pervading organisms.[3]

> But the character of an environment is the sum of the characters of the various societies of actual entities which jointly constitute that environment (PR 168-69).

> Thus instinct, or this immediate adjustment to immediate environment, becomes more prominent in its function of directing action for the purposes of the living organism. The world is a community of organisms; these organisms in the mass determine the environmental influence of any one of them; there can only be a persistent community of persistent organisms when the environmental influence in the shape of instinct is favourable to the survival of the individual. Thus the community as an environment is responsible for the survival of the separate individuals which compose it; and these separate individuals are responsible for their contributions to the environment. Electrons and molecules survive because they satisfy this primary law for a stable order of nature in connection with given societies of organisms (S 79).

> The main line of thought has been (i) that each actual occasion has at the base of its own constitution the environment from which it springs (PR 314).

> The concept of matter presupposed simple location. Each bit of matter was self-contained, localized in a region with a passive, static network of spatial relations, entwined in a uniform relational system from infinity to infinity and from eternity to eternity. But in the modern concept the group of agitations which we term matter is fused into its environment. There is no possibility of a detached, self-contained local existence. The environment enters into the nature of each thing. Some elements in the nature of a complete set of agitations

may remain stable as those agitations are propelled through a changing environment. But such stability is only the case in a general average way. This average fact is the reason why we find the same chair, the same rock, and the same planet, enduring for days, or for centuries, or for millions of years. . . . The fundamental fact, according to the physics of the present day, is that the environment with its peculiarities seeps into the group-agitations which we term matter, and the group-agitations extend their character to the environment. In truth, the notion of the self-contained particle of matter, self-sufficient (within its local habitation, is an abstraction (MT 188-89).

The character of an actual entity is finally governed by its datum. . . . It follows from this doctrine that the character of an organism depends on that of its environment (PR 168).

It is the accepted doctrine in physical science that a living body is to be interpreted according to what is known of other sections of the physical universe. This is a sound axiom; but it is double-edged. For it carries with it the converse deduction that other sections of the universe are to be interpreted in accordance with what we know of the human body (PR 181-82).

For the environment automatically develops with the species, and the species with the environment (SMW 161).

(2) "environment" as order necessary to sustain order.[4]

The main line of thought has been . . . (iii) that any actual occasion belonging to an assigned species requires an environment adapted to that species, so that the presupposition of a species involves a presupposition concerning the environment (PR 314).

Thus a society is, for each of its members, an environment with some element of order in it. . . .
But there is no society in isolation. Every society must be considered with its background of a wider environment of actual entities, which also contribute their objectifications to which the members of the society must conform. Thus the given contributions of the environment must at least be permissive of the self-sustenance of the society. Also in proportion to its importance, this background must contribute those general characters which the more special character of the society presupposes for its members. But this means that the environment, together with the society in question, must form a larger society in respect to some more general characters than those defining the society from which we started. Thus we arrive at the principle that every society requires a social background of which it is itself a part. In reference to any given society the world of actual entities is to be conceived as forming a background in layers of social order, the defining characteristics becoming wider and more general as we widen the background. Of course, the remote actualities of the background have their own specific characteristics of various types of social order.

47

But such specific characteristics have become irrelevant for the society in question by reason of the inhibitions and attenuations introduced by discordance, that is to say, by disorder (PR 138).

Accordingly, the key to the mechanism of evolution is the necessity for the evolution of a favorable environment, conjointly with the evolution of any specific type of enduring organisms of great permanence. Any physical object which by its influence deteriorates its environment, commits suicide (SMW 160-62).

Also survival requires order, and to presuppose survival, apart from the type of order which that type of survival requires, is a contradiction. It is at this point that the organic philosophy differs from any form of Cartesian 'substance-philosophy.' For if a substance requires nothing but itself in order to exist, its survival can tell no tale as to the survival of order in its environment. Thus no conclusion can be drawn respecting the external relationships of the surviving substance to its future environment. For the organic philosophy, anticipation as to the future of a piece of rock presupposes an environment with the type of order which that piece of rock requires (PR 311-12).

(3) "environment" as the totality of concrete actuality.[5]

As the subject-matter of a science expands, its relevance to the universe contracts. For it presupposes a more strictly defined environment.

The definition of the environment is exactly what is omitted from special abstraction. Such a definition is an irrelevance. It is irrelevant because it requires an understanding of the infinitude of things. It is therefore impossible. All that we can do is to make an abstraction, to presuppose that it is relevant, and to push ahead within that presupposition.

This sharp division between the clarity of finite science and the dark universe beyond is itself an abstraction from concrete fact (MT 77).

It follows that in every consideration of a single fact there is the suppressed presupposition of the environmental coordination requisite for its existence. This environment, thus coordinated, is the whole universe in its perspective to the fact (MT 13).

Senses (1) and (2) seem to be another mode of stating the reciprocity of whole and parts. They are referring to the internal relatedness of organism and environment. The order of the environment is determined by the organisms it sustains and the organisms could not remain in (that state of) existence without the order provided by that environment. Each is what it is because of its relationship to the other. Further, what constitutes an environment on one level of abstraction may be an organism to a wider environment. That is, it may contribute to the characteristics

48

of wider environments whose order is necessary for its continued existence. The implication is that there are layers of environmental order.

Sense (3) of "environment" is also bound up with the doctrine of internal relations. It expresses a recognition of the objection frequently raised against this doctrine that knowledge becomes impossible: all organisms are what they are by virtue of their relations to each other; hence knowledge of all organisms is presupposed in the knowledge of any one.[6] In view of this difficulty Whitehead speaks of the "irrelevance" of the "definition of the environment." His use of "irrelevant" requires clarification. He cannot mean that the environment is irrelevant to the existence of the organisms it supports or to the wider environments to whose characteristics it contributes. He uses the term, rather, to indicate the methodological necessity of limiting our consideration of environmental influence to finite regions.[7]

> The background in which an environment is set must be discriminated into two layers. There is first the relevant background, providing a massive systematic uniformity. This background is the presupposed world to which all ordinary propositions refer. Secondly, there is the more remote chaotic background which has merely an irrelevant triviality, so far as concerns direct objectification in the actual entity in question. This background represents those entities in the actual world with such perspective remoteness that there is even a chaos of diverse cosmic epochs (PR 171).

> Each actual occasion objectifies the other actual occasions in its environment. This environment can be limited to the relevant portion of the cosmic epoch. It is a finite region of the extensive continuum, so far as adequate importance is concerned in respect to individual differences among actual occasions. Also, in respect to the importance of individual differences, we may assume that there is a lower limit to the extension of each relevant occasion within this region. With these two presumptions, it follows that the relevant objectifications, forming the relevant data for any one occasion, refer to a finite sample of actual occasions in the environment (PR 313).

> The fashionable notion that the new physics has reduced all physical laws to the statement of geometrical relations is quite ridiculous. It has done the opposite. In the place of the Aristotelian notion of the procession of forms, it has substituted the notion of forms of process. It has thus swept away space and matter, and has substituted the study of the internal relations within a complex state of activity. This complex state is in one sense a unity. There is the whole universe of physical action extending to the remotest star-cluster. In another sense it is divisible into parts. We can trace inter-relations within a selected group of activities, and ignore all other activities. By such an abstraction, we

49

shall fail to explain those internal activities which are affected by changes in the external system which has been ignored. Also, in any fundamental sense, we shall fail to understand the retained activities. For these activities will depend upon a comparatively unchanging systematic environment (MT 192).

How, then, are we to understand a generic sense of "environment" underlying these three senses? It seems to me that the senses of "environment" may be expressed in the following meaning: "environment" refers to the order obtaining in a finite spatio-temporal region relevant to the existence of more special structures of order.[8] It is clear that Whitehead intended "environment" to be defined in terms of order. It is also clear that an environment is finite: this follows from his conception of order. Order and disorder are correlatives; order is never complete, merely dominant in some region.

> Now the correlative of 'order' is 'disorder.' There can be no particular meaning in the notion of 'order' unless this contrast holds. Apart from it, 'order' must be a synonym for 'giveness.' But 'order' means more than 'giveness," though it presupposes 'giveness,' 'disorder is also 'give' (PR 127).

> 'Order' is a mere generic term: there can only be some definite specific 'order,' not merely 'order' in the vague. Thus every definite total phase of 'givenness' involves a reference to that specific 'order' which is its dominant ideal, and involves the specific 'disorder' due to its inclusion of 'given' components which exclude the attainment of the full ideal. The attainment is partial, and thus there is 'disorder;' but there is some attainment, and thus there is some 'order.' There is not just one ideal 'order' which all actual entities should attain and fail to attain (PR 128).

It is the reference of order to a finite region that constitutes the justification of setting limits to a consideration of environmental influences.

In this chapter the concept of organic mechanism which is central in SMW and is developed into the philosophy of organism in PR, AI, and MT has been elucidated. This concept emphasizes the rejection of a materialistic mechanism, one characterized by understanding the behavior of wholes in terms of the behavior of its externally related parts. Materialistic mechanism is replaced with a mechanism in which the whole in some sense determines the behavior of the parts. The basic assumption of this organic mechanism is the internal relatedness of whole and part, such that (1) there is a reciprocal determination of part and whole and (2) the relationships of parts in any given whole is constitutive

50

of the parts. From this it follows that the minimum fundamental categories for understanding science are organism—any organic unity, i.e., a unity in which the unity is constituted by the determination of part by whole, and environment—any order necessary to maintain the existence of the organisms in question.

IV. The Order
of Nature

10. The problem of societies

The aim of this chapter is to investigate the range of applicability of the categories of organism and environment. In particular the subject of inquiry is whether or not the complex orders of nature which Whitehead calls "societies" can be handled by these categories. The inquiry is necessitated by a distinction which Whitehead makes between "societies" and "primary organisms." In SMW Whitehead raises the question "as to whether there are not primary organisms which are incapable of further analysis" and answers that "it seems very unlikely that there should be any infinite regress in nature" (SMW 150-51). Whitehead describes the primary organisms as events.

> Accordingly, a non-materialistic philosophy of nature will identify a primary organism as being the emergence of some particular pattern as grasped in the unity of a real event. Such a pattern will also include the aspects of the event in question as grasped in other events, whereby those other events receive a modification, or partial determination. . . . The concept of organism includes, therefore, the concept of the interaction of organisms (SMW 151).

In the mature philosophy of organism Whitehead drops the term event in favor of the category of "actual occasion." Actual occasions are the primary organisms.

Whitehead terms a set of actual occasions (primary organisms) which are involved with one another by a prehensive relationship a "nexus." Nexūs which have social order are "societies." Social order is strictly defined by Whitehead as being governed by three conditions: (1) an analogy or similarity condition—every actual occasion (primary organism) in society S has a common defining characteristic (call it A), (2) a genetic condition—A characterizes each actual occasion (primary organism) in S because of its prehension of antecedent members of the nexus (members characterized by A), and (3) a reproductive condition—

A is a positive prehension; that is, A is the defining character decided for by the acting actual occasions (primary organisms). A is thereby continued as the defining characteristic of the actual occasions (primary organisms) of S (PR 50-51).

The principal issue is whether or not both primary organisms and societies can be conceived as falling under the category of organism described in section 8, i.e., as characterized in terms of modification by the whole (primary organism or society). One can find passages in Whitehead's discussion of societies which support both views. It seems, therefore, that the resolution of the issue depends on finding a model for interpreting Whitehead's discussion of societies and attempting to put the passages into this general context.

11. A model for understanding societies

At the beginning of the discussion of societies in PR, even prior to setting out the conditions for social order, Whitehead states that the discussion is about the " 'order of nature,' meaning thereby the order reigning in that limited portion of the universe, or even of the surface of the earth, which has come under our observation" (PR 136). At this point he refers to three works by L. J. Henderson which he believes to be fundamental for discussing this order of nature.[1] A consideration of Henderson's general arguments in these works will, I believe, provide a context for understanding Whitehead's discussion of social order in the successive pages of PR. In the remainder of this section (11) the terms "organism" and "environment" are meant in their ordinary biological usage and not in the stretched senses of sections 8 and 9.

In *The Fitness of the Environment*, Henderson undertakes a study of the general relationship between organisms and their environment. He argues that the properties of matter exhibit a different order when considered dynamically than the order exhibited when considered statically, *viz.:*

> The properties of matter are not evenly distributed among the elements, nor in such a manner as can be explained by the laws of chance, nor are they altogether distributed in the manner which the periodic system describes. If the

53

extremes be considered, all the physical and chemical properties are distributed with the very greatest unevenness, so that the extremes are concentrated upon a few elements, notably hydrogen, oxygen and carbon. As a result of this fact there arise certain characteristics of the cosmic process which could not otherwise occur.[2]

This order is of the utmost importance to understanding the notion of biological fitness. This is because this order implies that the physico-chemical constitution of the surface of this planet (or any planet with the same or very similar physico-chemical constitution) assures (1) maximal stability of physico-chemical conditions, (2) maximal complexity of physico-chemical constituents, and (3) greatest potentiality for physico-chemical systems of maximal complexity, durability, and activity. Henderson argues that since characteristics (1)-(3) are essential to the evolution of living things, part of the meaning of biological fitness must be the fitness of the physico-chemical environment for life. In addition, since the physico-chemical character of this planet guarantees the maximization of all these characteristics, this environment can be considered the *fittest.*[3]

Henderson then generalizes the argument. The generalization is based on the fact that the characteristics in question are physico-chemical ones and not exclusively biological. The generalized argument is as follows: for any active system,[4] the environment which favors maximal durability and activity for the widest range of material systems is fittest. Since only the physico-chemical characters of the environment were considered and were found to meet the required condition, this environment is fittest for active systems generally.[5]

Henderson then generalizes the argument. The generalization is based on the fact that the characteristics in question are physico-chemical ones and not exclusively biological. The generalized argument is as follows: fittest for life; organisms, however, can increase in fitness. Henderson concludes that biological fitness is reciprocal. On the one hand the physico-chemical environment imposes conditions on organisms and is thereby active; on the other hand organisms are active in adapting to particular environments.[6]

The question then arises as to the origin of the two kinds of fitness. Henderson rejects the concept of dual origin: "The simplest view would be to imagine one common impetus operating upon all matter, inorganic and organic, through all stages of its evolution."[7] This constitutes a rejection of any vitalistic hypothesis; no claim is made with respect to unique characteristics for living things. Teleology, however, is a fundamental presupposition.[8]

The Order of Nature is an inquiry into organism as the guiding principle of the biological sciences. What are especially important for this discussion are Henderson's remarks on adaptability in the Preface. We have just seen that adaptability is an activity of organisms and that such adaptability constitutes one side of biological fitness. However in *The Order of Nature* Henderson also claims complete generality for adaptability. That is to say, adaptability is a physico-chemical problem, not an activity exclusive to life.[9] "For beneath all the organic structures and functions are the molecules and their activities. These it is that have been moulded by the process of evolution, and these no less have formed the environment."[10] The fundamental question then becomes: "What are the physical and chemical origins of diversity among inorganic and organic things, and how shall the adaptability of matter and energy be described?"[11] If adaptability is not unique to organisms, then this activity can be generalized to any physico-chemical system relating to its environment. This suggests the general relationship between whole and part in organic unities as described by Whitehead as well as the extension of the usual meanings of the terms organism and environment.

12. The order of nature

The conclusions of Henderson's arguments which are fundamental for discussing the order of nature for Whitehead, i.e., social order, can be summarized as follows. First, there is the reciprocity of biological fitness: the fitness of the environment amounts to the order of the environment which allows for more particular order to be sustained and to evolve; the fitness of organisms amounts to their adaptation to specific environmental orders. It is important that this conclusion can be stated in general terms about order. Such a statement stretches the ordinary biological uses of the terms organism and environment. This is because fitness is not exclusive to biology. Indeed the essential concepts for the fitness of organisms and the environment—survival, evolution, and adaptation—are applicable to the physico-chemical constituents of nature as well. This implies that "biological" fitness is the general model for understanding the order of nature. Second, the application of adaptation to the understanding of physico-chemical entities suggests hierarchical order in nature. That is, physico-chemical entities exhibit the fitness which is characteristic of organisms, *viz.*, adaptation, and can thus be conceived as organisms to some more general environment which allows for their survival and evolution. This leads to the hierarchical order discussed in sections 8 and 9: organisms considered on a particular level can act as an environment to sustain organisms at a lower level, and an environment considered on a particular level can be considered as an organism to a higher level environmental order. These two conclusions are in full agreement with the stretched meanings of organism and environment described in Chapter III.

Let us now turn to the issue of social order and attempt to relate Whitehead's discussion of societies to the generalized concepts of bio-logical fitness.

Whitehead frequently describes a society as an environment for its constituent actual occasions (primary organisms). "Thus a society is, for each of its members, an environment with some element of order in it, persisting by reason of the genetic relations between its own members. Such an element of order is the order prevalent in the society" (PR 138). Further, he maintains a layering of societies in such a manner that for any particular society there are wider societies which provide an environment for the member society.

> But there is no society in isolation. Every society must be considered with its background of a wider environment of actual entities, which also contribute their objectifications to which the members of the society must conform. Thus the given contributions of the environment must at least be permissive of the self-sustenance of the society. Also, in proportion to its importance, this background must contribute those general characters which the more special character of the society presupposes for its members. But this means that the environment, together with the society in question, must form a larger society in respect to some more general characters than those defining the society from which we started. Thus we arrive at the principle that every society requires a social background, of which it is itself a part. In reference to any given society

> the world of actual entities is to be conceived as forming a background in layers of social order, the defining characteristics becoming wider and more general as we widen the background (PR 138).

This passage has been cited above (section 9) in connection with the meaning of environment as the order necessary to sustain order. A society can, then, function as an environment, and in this function it possesses fitness in the sense that its order allows the orders for which it is an environment to survive.

Whitehead classifies societies into different categories (PR 151). The fundamental physico-chemical constituents of the surface of the earth (those which Henderson claims make this environment fittest: hydrogen, oxygen, carbon, water, carbonic acid) fall under the classification of "structured" societies. A structured society is one having a hierarchical organization. It contains and "provides an environment for" "subordinate societies" and "subordinate nexūs" in structured interrelationships.[12] By providing an environment a structured society sustains the order of its subordinate societies and nexūs. In addition structured societies are themselves set in a more general environmental society.

Living organisms constitute a special kind of structured society. Unlike other structured societies, they always require the special protection of inorganic societies.

> Thus a living society involves nexūs which are 'inorganic,' and nexūs which are inorganic do not need the protection of the whole 'living' society for their survival in a changing external environment. Such nexūs are societies. But 'entirely living' nexūs do require such protection, if they are to survive. According to this conjectural theory, an 'entirely living' nexus is not a 'society.' . . . A complex inorganic system of interaction is built up for the protection of the 'entirely living' nexūs, and the originative actions of the living elements are protective of the whole system. On the other hand, the reaction of the whole system provides the intimate environment required by the 'entirely living' nexūs. We do not know of any living society devoid of its subservient apparatus of inorganic societies (PR 157).

Whitehead's reference to *Blood* indicates that he is conceiving of these inorganic societies as possessing environmental fitness as Henderson describes it. Consider Henderson's example in Chapter I:[13]

> Protoplasm is a system of exquisite sensitiveness. In order that it may survive it must be protected from too great, or too rapid, or too irregular fluctuations in the physical, physico-chemical, and chemical conditions of the environment.

> Stability may sometimes be afforded by the natural environment, as in sea water. In other cases an integument may sufficiently temper the external changes. But by far the most interesting protection is afforded, as in man and higher animals, by the circulating liquids of the organism, the blood plasma and lymph. . . . There can be no doubt that the cells of warm-blooded animals are bathed by liquids of quite exceptional stability of composition and of physico-chemical properties, so that their protoplasm is in general not obliged to protect itself, if one may use such an expression. Needless to say, protoplasm is also otherwise protected. Thus it is often covered with a cell membrane which is not permeable to all substances and may manifest selective permeability even toward similar molecules.

The above discussion makes it sufficiently clear that the category of environment (as elaborated in section 9) is adequate to account for certain characteristics of societies. It remains to consider whether or not the category of organism (section 8) is sufficient to account for the remaining societal characteristics.

The environmental characteristics of societies have been shown in a discussion in which societies have been statically conceived. A consideration of societies as dynamic will reveal the other side of environmental fitness, fitness for evolution, and the fitness of organisms, adaptation.

Whitehead maintained that social order is in process.

> But there is not any perfect attainment of an ideal order whereby the indefinite endurance of a society is secured. A society arises from disorder, where 'disorder' is defined by reference to the ideal for that society; the favourable background of a larger environment either itself decays, or ceases to favour the persistence of the society after some stage of growth: the society then ceases to reproduce its members, and finally after a stage of decay passes out of existence (PR 139).

With respect to structured societies we have seen that they contain subordinate societies and are contained in more general environmental societies. This involves all structured societies in a survival game as this wider environment changes its features in certain respects. Structured societies can, accordingly, act in two ways.

First they can "specialize" themselves by exhibiting the sort of characteristics that will be in line with the changing environment (PR 153). Specialization is clearly an instance of fitness in the sense of adaptation. Hence structured societies which specialize are organisms adapting to particular environments.

Second, structured societies can remain "unspecialized," yet survive in one of two ways. Whitehead's description of these ways is important to understanding the adaptation of societies and warrants citing.

> One way is by eliciting a massive average objectification of a nexus, while eliminating the detailed diversities of the various members of the nexus in question. This method, in fact, employs the device of blocking out unwelcome detail. It depends on the fundamental truth that objectification is abstraction. It utilizes this abstraction inherent in objectifications so as to dismiss the thwarting elements of a nexus into negative prehensions. At the same time the complex intensity in the structured society is supported by the massive objectifications of the many environmental nexūs, each in its unity as *one* nexus, and not in its multiplicity as *many* actual occasions (PR 154).

> The second way of solving the problem is by an initiative in conceptual prehensions, i.e., in appetition. The purpose of this initiative is to receive the novel elements of the environment into explicit feelings with such subjective forms as conciliate them with the complex experiences proper to members of the structured society. Thus in each concrescent occasion its subjective aim originates novelty to match the novelty of the environment (PR 155).

Societies, then, can exhibit fitness by three kinds of adaptation—specialization, averaging, and conceptual initiative.

Specialization, averaging, and conceptual initiative are instances of organismic fitness as opposed to environmental fitness. Whitehead here is in complete agreement with Henderson that organismic fitness is a concept applicable to physico-chemical systems as well as biological ones. He, too, refers to the evolution of physico-chemical entities.

> The material universe has contained in itself, and perhaps still contains, some mysterious impulse for its energy to run upwards. This impulse is veiled from our observation, so far as concerns its general operation. But there must have been some epoch in which the dominant trend was the formation of protons, electrons, molecules, the stars (FR 24).

The organismic fitness of societies, however, raises a problem with respect to Whitehead's definition of social order in terms of analogy, genetic and reproductive conditions. The difficulty is this. A is the defining character of society S because every member of S inherits A from antecedent members of S. In other words the defining character of the primary organisms is A, and this determines the defining character of S as A. Yet in adaptation the emergence of novel defining characters B_i's is being emphasized. It remains a mystery why a society has defining

59

character B when its defining character is due to its constituent primary organisms, which are prehending A. It seems to me that the conditions which Whitehead lists for social order are not sufficient. The emerging character B can only be accounted for by the reciprocal acting of a society and its constituent primary organisms. Only in this situation is a society acting as a unity in a way that can lead to emergent properties.

Although he places extreme emphasis on genetic inheritance from the antecedent members of a society, Whitehead also recognizes that this doctrine abstracts from the internal relatedness of any society and the wider societies which form its environment. That is to say, the genetic inheritance which is a defining character of social order is always an inheritance modified by the acting of the wider social environment on the inheritance.

> Then physical endurance is the process of continuously inheriting a certain identity of character transmitted throughout a historical route of events. This character belongs to the whole route, and to every event of the route. This is the exact property of material. . . . Only if you take *material* to be fundamental, this property of endurance is an arbitrary fact at the base of the order of nature; but if you take *organism* to be fundamental, this property is the result of evolution.
>
> It looks at first sight, as if a physical object, with its process of inheritance from itself, were independent of the environment. But such a conclusion is not justified. For let B and C be two successive slices in the life of such an object, such that C succeeds B. Then the enduring pattern in C is inherited from B, and from other analogous antecedent parts of its life. It is transmitted through B to C. But what is transmitted to C is the complete pattern of aspects derived from such events as B. These complete patterns include the influence of the environment on B, and on the other antecedent parts of the life of the object. Thus the complete aspects of the antecedent life are inherited as the partial pattern which endures throughout all the various periods of the life. Thus a favourable environment is essential to the maintenance of a physical object (SMW 159-60).

It would seem that Whitehead understood the essential nature of the acting of the social environment to be the sending of information to the constituents of a society to affect adaptation to that particular society and to the wider social environment of which it is a part. But this amounts to a modification of the primary organisms of a society by a society itself. Since such a modification is the defining characteristic of an organic unity, societies can be conceived as organic unities and, thereby, organisms in the sense of section 8.

In conclusion, the very concept of reciprocal fitness has led to a stretching of the ordinary meanings of organism and environment in such a way that they are tantamount to the categories of organism and environment elaborated in sections 8 and 9. A consideration of societies in the light of reciprocal fitness has shown that the categories of organism and environment are indeed adequate to account for the order and activity of societies. Societies are environments to their constituent primary organisms and, as such, play a role in the survival and evolution of the order of nature. Societies are also organisms because there is modification in the adaptation of primary organisms to the society as a whole in the evolution of the order of nature.

V. Foundational Concepts and Evolution

13. The incoherence of materialism

One requirement which Whitehead places on scientific and metaphysical theories is that of coherence of the concepts of the speculation. "'Coherence,' as here employed, means that the fundamental ideas, in terms of which the scheme is developed, presuppose each other so that in isolation they are meaningless" (PR 5). Coherence does not require that the fundamental concepts are definable in terms of each other; rather they are interrelated, i.e., they presuppose each other or necessarily involve each other. "Incoherence," on the other hand, is "the arbitrary disconnection" of the fundamental concepts (PR 9). By "disconnection" Whitehead means that the fundamental concepts do not have a necessary relationship to one another—are not involved with one another. By "arbitrary" he is emphasizing that there is no understanding of the disconnection. Understood disconnection is not incoherent.

Whitehead maintained that metaphysics is the ground for interpreting the coherence of a scientific theory. This is because the fundamental concepts of a metaphysical system are more general than those of a scientific theory. More general concepts can show the connection or disconnection of less general concepts.

> The progress of science has now reached a turning point. The stable foundations of physics have broken up: also for the first time physiology is asserting itself as an effective body of knowledge, as distinct from a scrapheap. The old foundations of scientific thought are becoming unintelligible. Time, space, matter, material, ether, electricity, mechanism, organism, configuration, structure, pattern, function, all require reinterpretation. What is the sense of talking about a mechanical explanation when you do not know what you mean by mechanics? If science is not to degenerate into a medley of *ad hoc* hypotheses, it must become philosophical and must enter upon a thorough criticism of its own foundations (SMW 24).

Whitehead's remarks about evolution in a later chapter in SMW make a great deal more sense if they are read in the context of the above passage: the doctrine of evolution is in danger of becoming a set of *ad hoc* hypotheses because its foundational concepts have not been sufficiently analyzed. Some of the principal foundational concepts for evolution are among those listed by Whitehead as becoming unintelligible in view of developments in contemporary science—"mechanism," "mechanical explanation," "material," and "organism."

An analysis of these concepts will show why Whitehead claimed that the mechanisms of a materialistic philosophy are inadequate to account for evolution's "creative" side and that a materialistic philosophy is "incompatible" with a theory of evolution altogether. In addition it will make intelligible Whitehead's claim that a philosophy of organism has mechanisms which account for evolutionary development.

Let us consider the meanings Whitehead attached to the terms "material," "mechanism," "organism," and "evolution."

"Material": Whitehead equated the meaning of substance as material with what he termed the doctrine of "simple location."

> One such assumption underlies the whole philosophy of nature during the modern period. It is embodied in the conception which is supposed to express the most concrete aspect of nature. The Ionian philosophers asked, What is nature made of? The answer is couched in terms of stuff, or material—the particular name chosen is indifferent—which has the property of simple location in space and time, or, if you adopt the more modern ideas, in space-time. What I mean by matter, or material, is anything which has this property of *simple location*. By simple location I mean one major characteristic which refers equally both to space and to time, and other minor characteristics which are diverse as between space and time.
>
> The characteristic common both to space and time is that material can be said to be *here* in space and *here* in time, or *here* in space-time, in a perfectly definite sense which does not require for its explanation any reference to other regions of space-time. Curiously enough this character of simple location holds whether we look on a region of space-time as determined absolutely or relatively. For if a region is merely a way of indicating a certain set of relations to other entities, then this characteristic, which I call simple location, is that material can be said to have just these relations of position to the other entities without requiring for its explanation any reference to other regions of position to the same entities. In fact, as soon as you have settled, however you do settle, what you mean by a definite place in space-time, you can adequately state the relation of a particular material body to space-time by saying that it is just there,

in that place; and, so far as simple location is concerned, there is nothing more to be said on the subject (SMW 71-72).

"Organism": By "organisms," we have seen that Whitehead meant wholes which determine as well as are determined by their parts because the parts are modified by the pattern of the whole.

"Evolution": At least three theses are involved in the meaning of evolution. They report the empirical evidence of the development of complex from less complex organisms, the survival of species of organisms which do survive, and the extinction of species which have become extinct.

> But the whole point of the modern doctrine is the evolution of the complex organisms from antecedent states of less complex organisms (SMW 157).

> The evolutionary theory is nothing else than the analysis of the conditions for the formation and survival of various types of organisms (SMW 149).

> There are thus two sides to the machinery involved in the development of nature. On one side, there is a given environment with organisms adapting themselves to it. . . . From this point of view, there is a given amount of material, and only a limited number of organisms can take advantage of it (SMW 163).

"Mechanism" and "mechanical explanation": Unlike the terms "material," "organism," and "evolution," these terms do not receive an explicit characterization in Whitehead's discussion of evolution. He uses the terms indifferently with respect to both a materialistic philosophy and a philosophy of organism. The doctrine of simple location is materialistic mechanism, but, as we have seen, Whitehead also refers to "organic mechanism" (SMW 116, 156). For this reason, there seems to be no need to construe "mechanism" as a technical philosophical term. One meaning *(Shorter O.E.D.)* is a "system of mutually adapted parts working together; a piece of machinery; the machinery of some effect." I shall understand by "mechanism" the concept or set of concepts which suffices for the understanding of a particular observed effect (such as the development of more complex from less complex organisms, the survival and extinction of species). A mechanical explanation is one which gives such understanding.

This brief clarification of the meanings of these foundational concepts for evolution suffices to show the inadequacy of materialism to provide a mechanism for evolutionary development. The most important

64

inadequacy is with respect to the development of "complex organisms from antecedent states of less complex organisms." The failure comes about because of the meaning of materialism. A doctrine of materialism entails that all relationships are external. This is to say that what a thing (bit of material) is does not depend on its relationships to other things (bits of material); the relationships of a thing are not constitutive of it. The application of this doctrine to the formation of higher levels of order out of lower levels results in an aggregate view of the higher order. This means that when higher levels are formed out of lower levels of order there is no modification of the lower level to a pattern of the higher level. There is no modification of this kind because such modification requires that the relationships of the lower orders be constitutive of them. Materialism rules out the possibility of such internal relatedness. Yet increase in complexity depends upon such a modification. This is because there can be no real increase in complexity unless there is a new order brought about at the higher level. There can be no new order if what the lower orders are is independent of the relationships into which they enter. The formation of the higher order by their relationship does not bring about a new and independent order at all. The higher order is, in a sense, a misnomer. It is an aggregate and it cannot be said to be of greater complexity than its constituents.

The point I am attempting to make is that a necessary condition for evolution at all is an increase in complexity which cannot be accounted for on a materialistic view. It does not matter how many mechanisms are called upon—natural selection, mutation, etc. These mechanisms will be inadequate so long as they are attached *(ad hoc)* to a materialistic philosophy. They will be inadequate because the meaning of evolution and the meaning of materialism are incompatible. I take this to be Whitehead's point when he claims:

> In truth, a thoroughgoing evolutionary philosophy is inconsistent with materialism. The aboriginal stuff, or material, from which a materialistic philosophy starts is incapable of evolution. This material is in itself the ultimate substance. Evolution, on the materialistic theory, is reduced to the role of being another word for the description of the changes of external relations between portions of matter. There is nothing to evolve, because one set of external relations is as good as any other set of external relations. There can merely be change, purposeless and unprogressive (SMW 157).

Whitehead also claims that natural selection is an inadequate mechanism for the survival and extinction of species on the materialistic view. His argument is one that is frequently maintained by contemporary critics of neo-Darwinian interpretations of evolution, *viz.,* that this mechanism, upon inspection, reduces to a triviality. The tautologousness comes about when the mere fact of survival is taken to be a sufficient condition for fitness and adjustment to the environment and the mere fact of dying out a sufficient condition for maladjustment of an organism to its environment and for being unfit (FR 4-7). In general, the adjustment or maladjustment of an organism to its environment becomes useless as an explanatory category on a materialistic view. This is because both the organism and the environment are material and as such have only external relations to one another. "Evolution . . . is reduced to the role of being another word for the description of the changes of the external relations between portions of matter." The adjustment or maladjustment of organism to environment becomes, in effect, a description of an arbitrary change.

14. The coherence of organism

In discussing what would constitute adequate mechanisms for evolution, Whitehead does not exclude the mechanisms of the materialistic interpretation (SMW 163). Rather he emphasizes the need for the addition of mechanisms such as the following:[1]

1) the development of a favourable environment along with the endurance and development of organisms of the same species.

> Accordingly, the key to the mechanism of evolution is the necessity for the evolution of a favourable environment, conjointly with the evolution of any specific type of enduring organisms of great permanence. Any physical object which by its influence deteriorates its environment, commits suicide.
>
> One of the simplest ways of evolving a favourable environment concurrently with the development of the individual organism, is that the influence of each organism on the environment should be favourable to the *endurance* of other organisms of the same type. Further, if the organism also favours the *development* of other organisms of the same type, you have then obtained a mechanism of evolution adapted to produce the observed state of large multitudes of

analogous entities, with high powers of endurance. For the environment automatically develops with the species, and the species with the environment (SMW 160-1).

2) the development of a favourable environment by the endurance and development of organisms of associated species.

> It is evident, however, that I have explained the evolutionary mechanism in terms which are far too simple. We find associated species of living things, providing for each other a favourable environment. Thus just as the members of the same species mutually favour each other, so do members of associated species. We find the rudimentary fact of association in the existence of the two species, electrons and hydrogen nuclei. The simplicity of the dual association, and the apparent absence of competition from other antagonistic species accounts for the massive endurance which we find among them (SMW 162-63).

Both mechanisms refer to the necessity of a "favourable environment." At first glance, these mechanisms seem to be open to the same charge leveled by Whitehead at the mechanisms of a materialistic interpretation, *viz.*, triviality. However, a reminder of the meaning of "organism" and a consideration of the meaning of "environment" will show that these mechanisms do suffice to explain increasing complexity in evolutionary development as well as the survival and dying out of species.

"Organism" in the philosophy of organism is taken to mean the opposite of aggregate. It is a unity in which the parts are modified according to the pattern of the whole. This modification results in a new order. "Environment" is a correlative term. It refers to a more general order relevant to the existence of an organism or organisms. However, the character of this more general order is contributed to by the organisms it sustains. "Organism" and "environment," then, can be conceived as referring to different levels in a hierarchy. An environment at one level in the hierarchy can become an organism to a wider environment at a more general level. It is important to note that there is an internal relatedness between an organism and its environment. Their relationships are constitutive of each other. This internal relatedness is the factor on which the adequacy of the mechanisms of the organic philosophy turns.

Survival: The survival of a species is accounted for by an environment which sustains a species along with the proliferation of members of the species. This is due to the fact that the production and development of large numbers (a number large enough to have a dominant influence on environmental character yet not so large that the environment is incapable of sustaining) of similar organisms is productive of the environment itself. "The organisms can create their own environment. For this purpose, the single organism is almost helpless. The adequate forces require societies of coöperating organisms" (SMW 163-64). The survival of a species is thereby bound up with that species, contribution to the order necessary for its own maintenance.

Extinction: The dying out of species is accounted for because the deterioration of the environment of a species is at the same time the deterioration of the very order needed for its survival. It is an instance of the destruction of a hierarchical level by virtue of the collapse of order at a sustaining level.

Increasing complexity: Both organisms and their environments change. Where there is survival, order is not static; the organisms and the environment change together because of their internal relatedness. It is possible that, in this change, a new environmental order can arise which supports organisms which had not previously been capable of actually existing (because of an inadequate sustaining order). Herein lies the development of "complex organisms out of antecedent states of less complex organisms."

It seems, then, that the mechanisms Whitehead suggests are adequate ones for evolutionary development. (By adequate I do not mean complete.) Their adequacy is assured because in the philosophy of organism the concepts of organism, environment, and evolution involve each other. They are what Whitehead would call categories of a "coherent" system. The incoherence of the basic categories of materialism and evolution is the reason for the inadequacy of its mechanisms. However this is not to say that the mechanisms of natural selection, mutation, etc. are useless in general. They do have an explanatory role if they are taken conjointly with a philosophy of organism. This philosophy provides the conditions for their explanatory success. Taken conjointly with a materialistic philosophy, on the other hand, they can be considered *ad hoc* because of the fundamental incompatibility of materialism and evolution.

Part Three

METAPHYSICS
AND A
LOGIC OF
SCIENCE

VI. Contemporary Schools of Thought in the Philosophy of Science in the English-speaking World

15. Formalism and historical relativism

At present there is little agreement as to the number of schools of thought dominating the field of the philosophy of science. The most comprehensive study of these schools has as its aim the drawing of distinctions between the tradition of the English-speaking world and the continental tradition. This study recognizes one principal tradition in the English-speaking world, logical empiricism, whose goal is "to articulate an ideal of science for a group of disciples."[1] Five subgroups are listed within this general tradition according to the "primary interest" of each group: (1) Formalists—whose primary interest is "the ideal or improved language,"[2] (2) Oxfordists—whose primary interest is "ordinary language,"[3] (3) Reconstructionists—whose primary interest is "philosophical cosmology: the general nature of the universe,"[4] (4) Popperianists—whose primary interest is "human affairs," although another central concern is the growth or development of knowledge,[5] and (5) Pragmatists—whose primary interest is "man as agent—man as producer-of-science and as user-of-language."[6]

Other studies have ignored the Anglo-Saxon—continental division and have distinguished two schools in the English-speaking world. Although the division into two schools is made in different ways, there is a great deal of similarity in the outcome. One distinction that is made is between "logical positivism" and "the new philosophy of science."[7] The "new philosophy of science" is characterized as the "historical school."[8]

71

A second distinction is between "the Received View" and "the critics of it."[9] This division is based upon a criterion of theoretical understanding. "The Received View" is the logical positivist view of theories and theoretical understanding. A third view takes an understanding of scientific inference as the criterion for the division and terms the two schools "formalism" and "historical relativism."[10] In all three cases a division is made between the logical empiricist tradition ("logical positivism," "the Received View," "formalism") and its critics, who are in some sense concerned with a historical rather than a logical approach to the philosophy of science.

Part Three is concerned with a logic of science and hence will take the "formalist—historical relativist" distinction (based on logical inference) as the basis for discussion. It is fully recognized that the distinction is somewhat arbitrary, yet it will lend clarity to the discussion of the issues at hand.

The formalist school is the older tradition. Although members of this tradition[11] have rejected a thoroughgoing logical positivism, their position with respect to fundamental issues in the philosophy of science is in varying degrees indebted to positivistic doctrines. In general this school can be characterized by its acceptance of a logic of science; that is, its members maintain that there is a logic with respect to such scientific activities as the testing of theories, theoretical explanation, and conceptual change.

Historical relativism characteristically rejects a logic of science. The members of this tradition[12] base their discussion of fundamental methodological issues on arguments from historical examples. That is, with respect to those issues for which the formalist tradition describes a logic, these philosophers seem to deny the existence of a logical structure which transcends particular historical situations.

Many philosophers of science see merit in both traditions and cannot be placed within either. However among these thinkers few have seen the importance in explicating a general logic of science. One philosopher who has insisted on the value of such a logic is Mary Hesse. In a recent work[13] she has defended the attempt to explicate a logic of science on the grounds that its function is threefold: such a logic (1) provides criteria for "good science" and is thereby normative as well as descriptive, (2) as normative, can show the aim of methodology and the adequacy of methodologies in terms of fulfilling that aim, (3) has as its principal aim understanding, not the suggestion of research techniques.

I very much agree with Hesse regarding the value and function of a logic of science. At the same time I maintain that a logic of science cannot perform these roles unless it has itself received a grounding in a more general, *viz.,* metaphysical, theory.

At present there is a more positive attitude toward the value of metaphysics for the philosophy of science than at any other time in the past five decades. Three developments within the philosophy of science have led to this change in attitude toward metaphysics: (1) the logical positivists failed to make good their claim that metaphysical statements do not constitute a kind of knowledge. This claim was based on the untestability of metaphysical statements by experience. It is now generally recognized to be an unacceptable claim because any criteria which are adequate to marking off theoretical scientific statements as knowledge at the same time fail to exclude at least some metaphysical statements. This suggests the difficulty of formally demarcating metaphysical and theoretical scientific statements as different in kind. (2) Some philosophers of science who stand in the formalist tradition have admitted that although metaphysical theories can be demarcated from scientific theories, they are demarcated as a kind of knowledge distinct from scientific knowledge.[14] In addition they suggest that some metaphysical ideas have aided the advance of science.[15] (3) Some philosophers of science who stand outside the formalist tradition have insisted that there is a sense in which metaphysics is *essential* to good science. Two camps can be distinguished here. First, there are those who claim that metaphysics plays no role in normal scientific activity but that critical discussion of foundational concepts (i.e., metaphysical discussion) must take place when any field of science reaches a revolutionary state.[16] The function of such critical discussion is to reach agreement on a theory without which scientists cannot carry on their normal activity because of the lack of a common methodology. Second, there are those who maintain that metaphysical speculation is necessary for all periods of scientific activity because such speculation is necessary for the criticism of established theories.[17] It is necessary because alternative schemes will uncover new observations which allow for a criticism of established theories going beyond the observations determined to be relevant by the established theories themselves.

It seems to me that the roles for metaphysics suggested in (3) are of great importance for advance in the philosophy of science. However the full significance of the relation of metaphysics to the philosophy of science has not been recognized even by those who have found an essential role for metaphysics in science. This has resulted from an inadequate understanding of metaphysics. The use of the term "metaphysics" by those who maintain its essentiality is roughly equivalent to an account of an empirical situation which constitutes an alternative to the established theory.[18] The basic difficulty with this understanding of metaphysics is that it fails to attribute to metaphysics its full generality. I am suggesting that, although metaphysical and scientific theories differ only in degree and not in kind, emphasis on this difference in degree is of the utmost importance for understanding the relationship of metaphysics to the philosophy of science. Metaphysical theories differ from scientific theories in generality. Their increased degree of generality allows them to perform the functions suggested—that of determination of relevant observations and of criticism. But it is determination of relevance and criticism at a meta-level. Metaphysical theories are not to be conceived as alternatives to established scientific theories; rather they are systems on a level of generality higher than scientific theories. Metaphysical theories systematize the sciences themselves. In such a systematization the interconnection of scientific concepts is expressed. This interconnection provides a higher-level net for the recognition of relevant observations. The point is that, in general, theory precedes observation. Metaphysical theories can direct attention to certain types of observation and give significance to observations by fitting them into a system which provides an interpretation of them. This function is fundamentally the same as that suggested by the interpretation of metaphysics as an alternative account on the same level. The difference suggested is that an understanding of metaphysics as a more general theory allows a metaphysical theory to perform this role with increased efficiency. This comes about because although alternative theories on the same level can uncover new observations, they cannot provide a general understanding of their relevance. This general understanding depends upon an interpretation given by the interconnection of scientific concepts in a higher-level theory.

74

There is another respect in which theories on the same level of generality cannot be the critics of one another, *viz.,* in regard to the coherence of their concepts. Metaphysical theories conceived as more general theories, however, can criticize scientific concepts with respect to their coherence. The more general theory is required to judge whether or not the concepts involve one another. That is, since scientific theories are not theories of the highest generality, it is possible that their concepts involve presuppositions which are inconsistent on the highest level of generality. Only by judging a scientific theory in terms of a metaphysical system can such inconsistency be brought to the foreground.

These considerations suggest that the function of metaphysics in the philosophy of science is the understanding and grounding of scientific concepts and methodology. That is, the fundamental concepts of a metaphysical system should give an analysis of the foundational concepts of the sciences in such a way that these concepts themselves provide a grounding of the methodology of the sciences. The function of metaphysics is to provide an understanding in the most general sense.

The aim of Part Three is to develop a logic of science from the Whiteheadian concepts elaborated in Chapters III-V. By a "logic" of science I do not mean logic in the restricted sense of contemporary symbolic logic; rather I am referring to logic in the broad sense of the formal procedure of clarifying the status of such entities as laws of nature and of elucidating inference patterns involved in scientific methodology.

Chapters VII-XI will briefly sketch the formalist and the historical relativist positions with respect to the status of laws, the process of induction, the status of explanation, the process of conceptual change, and the process of reduction. Then I will develop a Whiteheadian position with respect to these issues. I will attempt to show that the Whiteheadian position provides a general logic which transcends particular historical examples and, at the same time, follows from the fundamental concepts of organism and environment elaborated in Part Two. This Whiteheadian position will be referred to as the organic view.

VII. Laws

16. Laws are true statements of universal (conditional) form

The formalist tradition in the philosophy of science has maintained some version of the view that a lawlike statement is of universal form, capable of being put into conditional form. A true lawlike statement is a law.[1] It is maintained, however, that such a characterization is inadequate to demarcate laws as different in kind from so-called accidental generalizations—propositions such as "All the men in this room are bald" and "All the screws in Smith's present car are rusty"—which are thought to be true merely "by accident." Hence a set of criteria are required to mark off laws from such accidental generalizations. It is generally agreed that the list of criteria supply some necessary, but not sufficient, conditions for demarcation.

Many criteria have been proposed for marking off laws from accidental generalizations. For our discussion it will suffice to consider five of the most frequently mentioned criteria, *viz.,*

(1) Laws are unlike accidental generalizations in that they make no reference to particular places, times, and objects, or are derivable from more fundamental laws which do not make such reference.[2]

(2) Laws are unlike accidental generalizations in possessing unrestricted generality.[3]

(3) Laws are unlike accidental generalizations in supporting subjunctive conditionals.[4]

(4) Laws are unlike accidental generalizations in supporting counterfactual conditionals.[5]

(5) Laws are unlike accidental generalizations in that they function differently (in an explanation) and we therefore have a different attitude towards them.[6]

A consideration of these criteria will be simplified if another kind of statement is added to this discussion—that of a biological generalization, such as "Albinotic mice always breed true" or "All living matter

76

contains DNA (or RNA)." Biological generalizations have been considered by some philosophers of science as different in kind from laws because of the failure they seem to share with accidental generalizations to meet the conditions for lawlikeness. Many points of similarity to accidental generalizations have been suggested, among them: biological generalizations are mere empirical generalizations;[7] biological generalizations always involve an implicit reference to a particular place and time;[8] biological generalizations apply to inhomogeneous rather than homogeneous classes.[9] The last two points are usually discussed in the context of genetic relationships.

I do not intend to discuss the difficulties already pointed out with respect to each of the above criteria;[10] I merely wish to discuss these criteria with respect to the concepts of organism and environment and their implications.

Criteria (1) and (2) are usually discussed together, and, indeed, they seem to amount to the same thing. According to the organic view I have been developing, these criteria cannot suffice to mark off laws from biological generalizations. This is because the concept of environment is completely general in nature: all organisms modify their environment and are modified by their environment. This is generally recognized for biological organisms, but it holds for physical and chemical organisms as well. Consider, for example, the relationship between the elementary particles and the various fields (electromagnetic, gravitational, etc.) of physics. The fields, which are defined over wide but finite regions, enter into the definitions of the particles and constitute part of the environment of the particles. Changes in the environment (fields) can bring about qualitative changes in the particles. At the same time the characters of the fields themselves are influenced by the particles. Hence there is a mutual relevance of organism (particle) and environment (field) not totally unlike that found on the biological level.[11]

Whitehead maintained the full generality of the concept of environment and recognized its application to physical as well as to biological organisms.

> We have seen that this fact of what the entities are in themselves is liable
> to modification by their environments. Accordingly the assumption that no
> modification of these laws is to be looked for in environments, which have
> any striking difference from the environments for which the laws have been

observed to hold is very unsafe. The physical entities may be modified in very essential ways, so far as these laws are concerned. It is even possible that they may be developed into individualities of more fundamental types . . . (SMW 156).

The point is that any organism requires an environment to sustain it, and the environment is a finite spatio-temporal region. It follows that (1) the organisms referred to in any biological generalization or law alike depend upon particular environments; (2) there is no warrant for extending a biological generalization or a law formulated about one environment to an environment with known different features or to one whose features we know nothing about. Hence there is no unrestricted generality of either biological generalizations or laws in the sense required by criterion (2). Further, a particular environment, hence a particular spatio-temporal region is always implicitly referred to, and this reference violates criterion (2).

An extension of this argument suffices to show that critera (1) and (2) fail to mark off laws from accidental generalizations as well.

The mention of particular places, times, and objects guarantees the restricted application of a proposition to a particular spatio-temporal region and thereby insures that the proposition has a restricted universality in some sense. All accidental generalizations refer to a particular spatio-temporal region—a very special environment. For example, the order which must obtain for a generalization such as "All the screws in Smith's present car are rusty" to hold true is very special indeed. But, as we have seen, all biological generalizations and laws refer to an environment as well. The environment is less special for biological generalizations and less special still for laws, but it is presupposed all the same. Hence there is an implicit reference to particular spatio-temporal regions of varying generality in all of these generalizations. It seems, then, that laws and accidental generalizations alike fail to meet criteria (1) and (2). Hence they cannot serve to distinguish laws from accidental generalizations.

Further, the interesting modifications of these criteria suggested by Nagel and Achinstein seem to be vulnerable to the same considerations.

Nagel replaces (1) with

(1)′ In the accidental universal, the objects of which the predicate . . . is affirmed (let us call the class of such objects the 'scope of predication' of the universal)

78

are severely restricted to things that fall into a specific spatiotemporal region. In the lawlike statement, the scope of predication of the . . . predicate . . . is not restricted in this way: . . . not required to be located in a fixed volume of space or a given interval of time.[12]

It is the case that the scope of predication of the predicate in a law is not as restricted as that of an accidental generalization. However there is no warrant for thinking this scope to be absolutely unrestricted. The existence of the objects constituting the scope of predication depends upon structures of order which are themselves defined over a restricted spatiotemporal region. Thus it seems that no law can have a predicate whose scope of predication is absolutely unrestricted. The cogency of (1)' depends on the interpretation of its description of lawlike universals as having predicates whose scope of predication is not restricted to mean that their scope of predication is less restricted than in the case of predicates of accidental generalizations. Although this is quite the case, it is a distinction in degree only and not one in kind.

Achinstein replaces (2) with the following criterion of generality:

(2)' A sentence is being used to express a restricted universal if it begins with a universal term, has a subject term, antecedent, and consequent conditions, and is being used to express a proposition a sufficient condition for whose truth is that each item that now actually satisfies the subject term and antecedent condition also satisfies the consequent condition. . . . Laws . . . that contain a subject term and antecedent and consequent conditions are general in the sense that they express unrestricted rather than restricted universals. They say something about all items satisfying the subject term and not just about those of these that do now, will later, or once did satisfy the antecedent condition.[13]

Accidental generalizations are, of course, restricted universals in Achinstein's sense. A sufficient condition for the truth of "All the screws in Smith's present car are rusty" is that each screw that actually is (was or will be) in Smith's car be rusty. A sufficient condition for the truth of a lawlike universal, on the other hand, is that anything which possibly satisfies the subject class and antecedent term also satisfies the consequent term.[14] Although (2)' indicates a distinction between laws and accidental generalizations, it is once again a distinction of degree and not of kind. Laws express universals less restricted than accidental generalizations.[15] In addition the sufficient condition for the truth of a lawlike universal depends on the implicit assumption of a static and universal environmental order—an assumption without sufficient warrant.

The distinction intended by criterion (3) can perhaps be clarified by considering the purported differences in the relationships between a law, a biological generalization, an accidental generalization, and their corresponding subjunctive conditionals. It is claimed, on the one hand, that "All freely falling bodies fall with constant acceleration" supports the subjunctive conditional "If a body were a freely falling body it would fall with constant acceleration." On the other hand the biological generalization "All ravens are black" does not support "If an organism were a raven, it would be black," and the accidental generalization "All the screws in Smith's present car are rusty" does not support "If a screw were a screw in Smith's present car it would be rusty."[16] Why do the biological and accidental generalizations fail to support the subjunctive conditionals? A variety of reasons have been suggested, but it seems to me that the concept of environment underlies these reasons: the failure comes about because the truth of the subjunctive conditional involves an environment wider than that to which the biological generalization and the accidental generalization are known to apply. It may well be that the conditions of this wider environment are capable of supporting counterinstances to the biological and accidental generalizations and hence these generalizations do not support conditionals about this wider environment.[17] This is to say that we believe the biological and accidental generalizations fail to support subjunctive conditionals because we believe we are unwarranted in extending these generalizations to environments for which we lack important information or to environments we believe to have importantly different features than the original environment under consideration.

However if we were making such an extension in the case of a law, we should have the same reservations. We believe the subjunctive conditional to be supported by the law only when we assume the environment presupposed by the law to be so encompassing as to include the case of the subjunctive conditional. Hence it seems that criterion (3) does not suffice to show that laws and accidental generalizations are different in kind.

The case is quite similar with criterion (4). Recent discussions of this criterion have clearly shown that whether or not a law or an accidental generalization supports a counterfactual conditional depends on a variety of assumptions that need to be made explicit before the truth of the counterfactual can be decided.[18] In certain contexts even accidental generalizations support counterfactual conditionals. One of the clearest examples has been given by Pap.

> Suppose we knew that Jones never put any coins other than nickels into his trouser pocket. We should then be inclined to infer that somehow he had acquired the habit of allocating different coins to different places, perhaps for reasons of expediency. In this case there would be an indirect causal connection between the location and character of Jones' coins. If someone claimed to have just found a dime that had dropped out of Jones' pocket, one might then quite reasonably protest, "Oh no, if it had been in Jones' trouser pocket it would have been a nickel, for Jones the pedant is never known to put any other coins into his trouser pockets. . . .[19]

To say that whether or not a counterfactual conditional is supported depends upon certain assumptions or certain contexts amounts to saying that support or nonsupport depends on the environment presumed. Frequently the environment presumed for the truth of the counterfactual conditional has strikingly different features from that of the accidental generalization called upon to support it. However since a law also would not support a counterfactual conditional under these conditions, the criterion cannot distinguish laws and accidental generalizations as different in kind.

The difference in our attitude towards laws and accidental generalizations referred to by criterion (5) is generally discussed in the context of the relationship of each to counterinstances. It is claimed that we do not easily abandon a law in the face of a counterinstance but readily give up an accidental generalization. There are a variety of "moves" one can make with regard to a law faced with counterinstantial evidence —e.g., there may be a modification of theoretical entities or a postulation of new ones to accommodate the counterinstances,[20] or restriction of the application of the law,[21] or a tendency to regard the law as an approximation.[22] The reasons given for nonabandonment are that the laws belong to the theory or that the nature of their support makes abandonment difficult. Both reasons are based on the underlying reason of systematic import.[23] Laws belong to a theory and thereby systematize other basic uniformities. Laws are based on support other than instances falling within the scope of predication of the law, *viz.*, confirming instances for laws which entail or are entailed by the law. Hence a law is not independent of other laws and its abandonment would require changes in these laws. In brief, the stubbornness with which we hold on to a law is an indication of its place in the body of scientific knowledge at a particular time.[24]

In contrast accidental generalizations do not systematize more basic uniformities and are not supported by the same variety of evidence as laws. Hence abandoning accidental generalizations does not require widespread modification because these generalizations lack the systematic import possessed by laws.

It remains to ask if this systematic import reflects a difference in kind between laws and accidental generalizations or if it is once again a matter of degree.

The systematizing power of a law depends, it would seem, on the environment presumed. We hesitate to abandon laws because for a particular environment they are useful in systematizing other uniformities. In another environment they may fail to systematize and, in such circumstances they would be very easily abandoned for that environment. But it is difficult to argue that a true accidental generalization does not systematize for any environment. An accidental generalization is a low-level generalization and does not ordinarily systematize other uniformities, but there is a sense in which it can usefully systematize phenomena in a special environment—the coins in Jones' pockets, the screws in Smith's present car, etc.

We abandon accidental generalizations easily because of the specialness of the environment presumed; our reluctance to abandon laws is based on their usefulness in an implicit wide environment. This perhaps becomes more clear when we ask how biological generalizations are to be regarded in relation to counterinstances. It can be argued that we do not easily abandon them so long as they are useful. Indeed some of the same "moves" available to physicists in holding on to laws for which counterinstances have been found are also available to biologists, e.g., restriction of application.[25]

Then it is difficult to see a distinction in kind between laws and accidental generalizations based on the notion of systematic import. Systematic import is relative to a particular environment, and the ease with which a generalization is abandoned depends on its usefulness and this, in turn, depends on the specialness of the environment.

This sampling of the criteria should make it clear that the distinction between laws, biological generalizations, and accidental generalizations is a difficult one to define. Each of these statements presupposes a particular set of environmental conditions in order to hold; and when the notion of environment is made explicit, the usual criteria do not suffice to distinguish between them. None of these general propositions is universal or unrestricted; none is truly necessary or nonaccidental. Laws are less restricted and less accidental than biological generalizations, and these in turn are less restricted and less accidental than accidental generalizations.

17. Laws are formal statements (neither true nor false) in accordance with which we draw inferences about phenomena

It is difficult to sketch a historical relativist position on laws of nature. The principal interest of this tradition has been that of elucidating a new theory of conceptual change; few attempts have been made in the direction of setting out a systematic philosophy of science. This is, of course, totally in line with the basic thesis of this school, *viz.,* that there is no logic of science which transcends particular historical situations. At the same time this thesis does not entail that an attempt to demarcate laws from other kinds of statements cannot or should not be made. One philosopher in this tradition who has done a great deal of work toward clarifying the status of laws is Stephen Toulmin. This section will summarize his account of laws. It cannot be concluded, however, that all historical relativists would agree with his view.[26]

Toulmin is in radical disagreement with the formalist position on laws. He rejects both defining characteristics of laws maintained by the formalists—true and of universal form—as being irrelevant to laws.

> Firstly, the propositions figuring within scientific theories never—except obliquely—tell us anything 'true' or 'false' about the aspects of the empirical world to which they apply. Secondly: such propositions cannot—in any straightforward manner—be fitted into the standard logical classifications, as 'universal' or 'particular' propositions. . . .[27]

Toulmin maintains that if the terms "true" and "false" were relevant to characterizing laws, we would be forced to the unhappy conclusion that all laws are false because all laws have a restricted range of application. He insists instead that it is in considering the application of a law that true and false statements become relevant. When "application" replaces "truth" in making a characterization of laws, the terms "universal" and "particular" become properly applied to "application" and not to the law itself. That is, laws are not to be defined as universal (or particular) statements. The relevant use of these terms is in relation to the universal or conditional application of the law. In putting the focus on application, Toulmin is displacing the terms "true" and "universal" to function in meta-statements about laws. "True" and "universal" are not characteristics of laws themselves.[28]

The distinction between a law and statements about its application provide Toulmin with a way of distinguishing laws from biological and accidental generalizations. Laws are not to be conceived of as having truth value; however corresponding to any law of nature is a set of statements about its scope which can be true or false.[29] This distinction does not apply to either biological or accidental generalizations. Biological generalizations, according to Toulmin, are simple empirical generalizations and, hence, are either true or false.[30] Accidental generalizations, also, are either true or false.[31]

A law, then, is "the form of a regularity"—a formal statement which is associated with a set of true/false, particular/universal statements about its scope.

In Toulmin's view laws function as tools for making inferences among the phenomena that fall within their scope.[32] This feature of laws will be considered in more detail in Chapter VIII.

Whitehead has also maintained that laws are neither true nor false.

> The formulae [Newton's] required limitation as to the scope of their application. This definition of scope has now been provided by recent formulae which in their turn will, in the progress of science, have their scope of application defined. Newton's formulae were not false: they were unguardedly stated. Einstein's formulae are not false: they are unguardedly stated. We now know how to guard Newton's formulae: we are ignorant of the limitations of Einstein's formulae. In scientific investigations the question, True or False?, is usually irrelevant. The important question is, In what circumstances is this formula true, and in what circumstances is it false? If the circumstances of truth be infrequent or trivial or unknown, we can say, with sufficient accuracy for daily

use, that the formula is false (FR 53).

Toulmin has, however, distinguished his position from Whitehead's. His interpretation of Whitehead is based upon the argument we have seen in section 16, *viz.,* there is no warrant for extending laws formulated about one environment to an environment with known different features or to an environment about which we know nothing. Toulmin takes this to mean that laws are "restricted generalizations"[33] and that therefore the question as to their truth is a relevant one.

The passage quoted from FR seems to suggest that Toulmin (or Kneale) has misinterpreted Whitehead. But the notion of "generalization" is admittedly vague. And a further difficulty for the organic view is raised by Toulmin's account. In section 16 we argued that the concept of environment made it difficult to distinguish laws as different in kind from biological and accidental generalizations. But clearly the notions of "truth" and "falsity" are relevant to accidental generalizations; yet we have just seen that Whitehead claims these notions are not relevant to laws. The difficulty can, I think, be overcome by a reconsideration of accidental generalizations, biological generalizations, and laws (and their respective environments) in relation to the notions of "truth" and "falsity" ("universality" and "particularity").

18. Laws are statements about dominant orders of general environments

Accidental generalizations are either true or false. They are true if every organism mentioned in the generalization can be so characterized and false otherwise. Their truth is bound up with the specialness of their environment. That is, the contribution of the organisms to the defining characteristics of the environment is of the nature of a class concept: If the generalization is true, each organism in the environment has the same relevant characteristic(s). A true accidental generalization is, in effect, descriptive of an environment without "disorder"; it represents a dominant order in a "Pickwickian" sense. It is dominant, but there is no "disorder." Indeed the environment could not tolerate any disorder and at the same time be described by a true accidental generalization. A false accidental generalization, on the other hand, no longer systematizes the organisms of the environment for which it is formulated in any important sense. The limited systematizing power of an accidental generalization depends, then, upon its being true.

The case is otherwise with respect to laws, and this difference constitutes a criterion for distinguishing laws from accidental generalizations. Laws, as well as accidental generalizations, depend upon the characteristics of the organisms in the environments for which they are formulated. Whitehead has expressed this feature of laws by the term "immanence."

> The laws are the outcome of the character of the behaving things: they are the 'communal customs.' . . . This conception should replace the older idea of given things with mutual behaviour conditioned by imposed laws. What we know of external nature is wholly in terms of how the various occasions in nature contribute to each other's natures. The whole environment participates in the nature of each of its occasions. Thus each occasion takes its initial form from the character of its environment. Also the laws which condition each environment merely express the general character of the occasions composing that environment. This is the doctrine of the definition of things in terms of their modes of functioning (AI 52).

> By the doctrine of Law as immanent it is meant that the order of nature expresses the characters of the real things which jointly compose the existences to be found in nature. When we understand the essences of these things, we thereby know their mutual relations to each other. Thus, according as there are common elements in their various characters, there will necessarily be corresponding identities in their mutual relations. In other words, some partial identity of pattern in the various characters of natural things issues in some partial identity of pattern in the mutual relations of those things. These identities of pattern in the mutual relations are the Laws of Nature. Conversely, a Law is explanatory of some community in character pervading the things which constitute Nature (AI 142).

Yet whereas laws are immanent, they represent the dominant order of an environment in a meaningful sense. They do so because of the element of disorder in wide environments.

> 'Disorder' is a relative term expressing the lack of importance possessed by the defining characteristics of the societies in question beyond their own bounds. When those societies decay, it will not mean that their defining characteristics cease to exist; but that they lapse into unimportance for the actual entities in question. The term 'disorder' refers to a society only partially influential in impressing its characteristics in the form of prevalent laws (PR 141-42).

But the character of an environment is the sum of the characters of the various societies of actual entities which jointly constitute that environment; although it is pure assumption that every environment is completely overrun by societies of entities. Spread through the environment there may be many entities which cannot be assigned to any society of entities. The societies in an environment will constitute its orderly element, and the non-social actual entities will constitute its element of chaos. There is no reason, so far as our knowledge is concerned, to conceive the actual world as purely orderly, or as purely chaotic (PR 168-69).

In contrast to accidental generalizations, the fact of disorder accounts for the irrelevance of the terms "true" and "false" (and "universal" and "particular") for laws. The dominant order referred to by a law can tolerate disorder up to a certain point and the law still systematize the organisms in its environment. That is, whereas for an accidental generalization the failure of the organisms to exhibit the relevant characteristic(s) referred to in the generalization renders it no longer applicable because it is false, the failure of many organisms, and even societies of organisms, to exhibit the relevant characteristics of the dominant order of the environment described by a law do not render that order inapplicable.

In the main it seems that Whitehead is in agreement with Toulmin. First, "truth" and "falsity" are not relevant to the characterization of laws; rather questions as to under what conditions (environments) they hold are relevant. Second, "universal" and "particular" are not relevant to the characterization of laws, rather the relevant issue is that of conditional or universal applicability. On the organic view, since an environment is a finite spatio-temporal region, all laws are conditionally applicable.

The organic characterization of biological generalizations with regard to "truth," "falsity," ("universal," "particular"), however, differs from Toulmin's account. Biological generalizations are also (meaningful) dominant orders of environments. As theoretical biology advances, there is reason to believe that biological generalizations will be formulated which range over increasingly wider environments. However, since biological organisms require more special environments than do physico-chemical organisms, there is no warrant for thinking that biological generalizations will ever represent dominant orders of environments as wide as those represented by the statements generally referred to as laws.

87

The remainder of this section will summarize the organic view of laws as thus far developed and draw some implications from the notions of disorder and immanence.

Laws are to be conceived as statements of the dominant characteristics of wide, or general, environments. The point at which an environment is wide enough for its dominant characteristics to be described as a law is more or less arbitrary. Any particular law is an abstraction of a dominant order on a certain level of generality from the total existing order. This is due to the fact that environment E is bound up with wider environments E*, E**, . . . whose characteristic features are not those dominant in E. But, in turn, the characteristic features of the wider environments are abstractions. Hence even the most general laws are not universal but represent a dominant character of a particular level of a hierarchy of order.

The facts of immanence and disorder entail two further characterizations of laws.

First, since there is disorder and laws represent merely the dominant order of an environment, all laws should be conceived as fundamentally statistical in character. They are the "communal customs," the "large average effects," the "average, regulative conditions" to which Whitehead refers.

> The exact conformation of nature to any law is not to be expected. If all the things concerned have the requisite common character, then the pattern of mutual relevance which expresses that character will be exactly illustrated. But in general we may expect that a large proportion of things do possess the requisite character and a minority do not possess it. In such a case, the mutual relations of these things will exhibit lapses when the law fails to obtain illustration. In so far as we are merely interested in a confused result of many instances, then the law can be said to have a statistical character. It is now the opinion of physicists that most of the laws of physics, as known in the nineteenth century, are of this character (AI 143).

> The universe is not a museum with its specimens in glass cases. Nor is the universe a perfectly drilled regiment with its ranks in step, marching forward with undisturbed poise. . . . Science deals with large average effects, important within certain modes of observation (MT 123).

> Now these simplest things are those widespread habits of nature that dominate the whole stretch of the universe within our remotest, vaguest observation. None of these Laws of Nature gives the slightest evidence of necessity. They are the modes of procedure which within the scale of our observations do in

fact prevail. I mean, the fact that the extensiveness of the Universe is dimensional, the fact that the number of spatial dimensions is three, the spatial laws of geometry, the ultimate formulae for physical occurrences. There is no necessity in any of these ways of behavior. They exist as average, regulative conditions because the majority of actualities are swaying each other to modes of interconnection exemplifying these laws (MT 211-12).

All social order depends on the statistical dominance in the environment of occasions belonging to the requisite societies. The laws of nature are statistical laws derived from this fact (PR 314-15).

Second, since laws are immanent and since an environment can become incapable of supporting the organisms it once supported, new dominant orders, capable of supporting new types of organisms, can arise. Then it is clear that an order can pass out of dominance and new orders can come into dominance. Laws are, in brief, capable of evolving.

But there is not any perfect attainment of an ideal order whereby the indefinite endurance of a society is secured. A society arises from disorder, where 'disorder' is defined by reference to the ideal for that society; the favourable background of a larger environment either itself decays, or ceases to favor the persistence of the society after some stage of growth: the society then ceases to reproduce its members, and finally after a stage of decay passes out of existence. Thus a system of 'laws' determining reproduction in some portion of the universe gradually rises into dominance; it has its stage of endurance, and passes out of existence with the decay of the society from which it emanates (PR 139).

In so far as there is large mutual conformity in the data, the energetic form of composition is such as to transmit this conformity to the issue, thereby preserving that uniformity for the future. We have here the bases of the large scale preservation of identities, amid minor changes. The plants, the stones, the living things all witness to the wide preservation of identity. But equally they witness to the partiality of such preservation. Nothing in realized matter-of-fact retains complete identity with its antecedent self. This self-identity in the sphere of realized fact is only partial. It holds for certain purposes. It dominates certain kinds of process. But in other sorts of process, the differences are important, and the self-identity is an interesting fable. . . . In so far as identities are preserved, there are orderly laws of nature. In so far as identities decay, these laws are subject to modification. But the modification itself may be lawful. The change in the individual may exhibit a law of change, as for example, the change from baby to fully-grown animal. And yet such laws of change are themselves liable to change. For example, species flourish and decay; civilizations rise and fall; heavenly bodies gradually form, and pass through sequences of stages.

> In any of these examples, as the changes occur, new types of existence are rendered possible, subject to new laws of nature dependent upon that new environment. In other words, the data, the forms of process, and the issues into new data, are all dependent upon their epoch and upon the forms of process dominant in that epoch (MT 129-30).

In summary, the organic view of laws conceives them as statements of dominant orders of environments. Since environments are finite spatio-temporal regions, laws are restricted and not universal. Because of the disorder in any environment, laws are essentially statistical in character. Finally, since laws are capable of evolving, they are non-necessary statements.[34] In contrast to the formalist view, the organic view does not hold "true" and "universal" to be characteristics of laws. Then there is no difficulty with respect to distinguishing laws from those accidental generalizations which are true and of universal form. The organic view is in agreement with the historical relativist view that it is the very characteristic of laws of not being true or false which suffices to distinguish them from accidental generalizations. However when the concepts of organism and environment are added to the analysis, the organic view takes issue with the historical relativist view with respect to the classification of biological generalizations. Biological generalizations as well as laws are statements about the environments of organisms; hence biological generalizations differ in degree but not in kind from physical laws.

VIII. Induction

19. The logic of science as deductive logic

On the whole formalists have given priority to deductive reasoning in science. They have regarded deductive logic as the only logic capable of receiving justification, and they have pointed out important reasons for calling the role of induction into question. These reasons all center around the justification of induction, but the arguments take several different forms. Three of the most important arguments relevant to discussing the organic view are offered by Hempel, Popper, and Goodman.

Hempel stresses the "nonmechanical" or "imaginative" aspect of hypothesis formation, which seems to preclude the use of induction. In general it is not possible to infer "by means of mechanically applicable rules from observed facts to corresponding general principles."[1] The main reason mechanical hypothesis formation is not to be found, or even to be expected, is the occurrence of new terms in theories which are not found in the observational data (or lower-level uniformities) on which they are based and which they systematize.

The kinds of mechanical induction meant must be simple enumeration of instances and/or canons, such as those given by Bacon and Mill. In generalization from the enumeration of instances there is no place for the introduction of new terms which occur in theories but not in the data upon which they are based. Likewise the methods of agreement, disagreement, concomitant variations, etc., do not allow for the introduction of new terms in the causal connection inferred. Indeed it is a standard objection to these methods that unless there is proper analysis of antecedent conditions based upon new concepts (expressed by new terms), the methods will not be successful; and the new concepts do not arise in the methods themselves.

A further difficulty is how the introduction of such new terms can be (logically) justified. If deduction is taken to be the only justifiable mode of inference, then it is clear that these terms cannot be introduced by any justifiable inference step.[2] It follows that there is no induction involved in hypothesis formation. For Hempel, then, a logic of hypothesis formation is to be replaced by noninferential inventions or guesses. "Scientific hypotheses and theories are not *derived* from observed facts, but *invented* in order to account for them. They constitute guesses at the connections that might obtain between the phenomena under study. . . ."[3]

Clearly Hempel is right about the following points.

(1) There are new concepts in theories which are not found in the observational data on which they are based and which they systematize.

(2) These concepts cannot be reached by "mechanical" inductive methods.

(3) The discovery of these concepts requires imagination.

Any adequate account of the role of induction in theoretical inference will have to take account of (1)-(3). At the same time (1)-(3) are not strong enough to support the claim that induction has no role to play in theoretical inference—in Hempel's terms they are not strong enough to imply that "inventions" are not reasonable. Hempel takes this into account and makes a distinction between "induction in a narrow sense" and "induction in a wide sense." The former refers to induction as the logic of hypothesis formation and is to be rejected. The latter refers to the acceptance of hypotheses on the basis of inferences which do not constitute valid deductive reasoning.[4] In effect the problem of induction is taken from the realm of discovery and placed in the context of confirmation theory. Hence Hempel's deductivism is supplemented by inductive logic for some areas of inference drawing in science, *viz.,* validation or confirmation.

Popper's radical rejection of induction in all areas of scientific inference is due to the inability of philosophers to answer the difficulties that Hume raised about induction. Popper has conceived this problem to be the justification of a general principle of induction (a principle which in conjunction with observational data could provide a deductive inference to the general conclusion). Popper argues that all possible ways of justifying such a principle lead to difficulties: an empirical justification involves an infinite regress; a metaphysical justification (one based on synthetic *a priori* categories) involves triviality or circularity.[5] The latter kind of justification raises special problems for the philosophy of organism, because the organic view is fully in accord with Whitehead's view as to the nature of metaphysical method. Whitehead maintained that metaphysical categories are "generalizations" from experience (PR 4-26). Indeed Whitehead did not make a distinction in kind between scientific and metaphysical method. The categories of both science and metaphysics are arrived at in the same way; the difference is that the metaphysical categories, but not the scientific, are fully general. Hence a certain kind of circularity does seem to arise. Induction is justified by categories themselves inductively reached.[6]

In face of the apparent insolubility of the justification of a general principle of induction, some formalists have limited the required justification to the role of induction in making valid inferences to predictions. Goodman has discussed this as the "new riddle of induction."

> The traditional smug insistence upon a hard-and-fast line between justifying induction and describing ordinary inductive practice distorts the problem.
>
> The problem of induction is not a problem of demonstration but a problem of defining the difference between valid and invalid predictions.[7]

The difficulty of justifying a general principle of induction and the shift made by Goodman (and Hempel, although not Popper) to a far more limited problem suggests an additional requirement for an adequate theory as to the role of induction, viz.,

(4) In any validation of induction the justification of a general principle of induction is not being sought but rather that of a "valid inductive inference" pattern.

All too frequently philosophers of science take the argument that a general principle of induction cannot be justified as a warrant for the thesis that there is no rational theory formation.[8] It seems to me that this thesis is not at all warranted. (4) leaves an important option for justifying "valid inductive inference" patterns to theories and to predictions.

20. Theory-ladenness and induction

The antiinductive stance of the historical relativists has been based on arguments quite different from those of the formalists. However just as the unifying thread of the formalists' arguments can be found in the problem of the justification of induction, there is a central problem from which the historical relativists' arguments stem. This is the theory-ladenness of observational meaning. A fundamental thesis that histori-cal relativists hold in common is the priority of theory to observation. One implication of this thesis is that the meaning of theoretical terms determines (in some sense) the meaning of observational terms and, therefore, a change or extension in a theory will affect the meaning of terms in the less general uniformities and phenomena they explain.

In part Toulmin's position on laws of nature derives from the thesis of theory-ladenness.[9] We have seen that he denies that laws are inductive generalizations (section 17) for two reasons. First, even when the same term occurs in the observational data and the law or principle— e.g., data about light and the principle that "Light travells in straight lines"—there is an extended use of the term "light" in the principle. It is, in this sense, a new concept, which becomes the occasion for the asking of questions—in effect the extended use of the term provides a new "inferring technique."

> Yet in the optical case, both the key words in our conclusion—'light' and 'travel-ling'—are given new uses in the very statement of the discovery. Before the discovery is made, the word 'light' means to us such things as lamps—the 'light' of "Put out the light"; and illuminated areas—the 'light' of "The sun-light on the garden." Until the discovery, changes in light and shade, as we ordinarily use the words (i.e. illuminated regions which move as the sun moves), remain things primitive, unexplained, to be accepted for what they are. After the discovery, we see them as the effects of something, which we also speak of in a new sense as 'light,' travelling from the sun or lamp to the illuminated objects. A crucial part of the step we are examining is, then, simply this: com-ing to think about shadows and light-patches in a new way, and in consequence coming to ask new questions about them, questions . . . which are intelligible only if one thinks of the phenomena in this new way.[10]

Second, laws and principles are unlike inductive generalizations be-cause generalizations are falsified by counterinstances whereas laws and principles are not. Again the difference turns on the extended use of the term in the case of the law or principle but not in the case of the induc-tive generalization. In the generalization the words are not given new senses. In the case of laws and principles counterinstances do not falsify, because the law or principle is not regarded as true or false in any proper sense at all, but as an inference technique.

> Nor is it the discovery that whatever is travelling, in the everyday sense, is

94

doing so in one way rather than another. . . . Often enough, as we soon find out, light does not travel strictly in straight lines, but is diffracted, refracted or scattered; yet, in practice, this in no way affects the point of the principle that light travells in straight lines. . . . Rather, the optical discovery is, in part at any rate, the discovery that one can speak at all profitably of something as travelling in these circumstances, and find a use for inferences and questions suggested by this way of talking about optical phenomena—the very idea that one should talk about anything as travelling in such circumstances being the real novelty.[11]

Toulmin's discussion is aimed at making sense of the notion of a discovery. He is claiming that a discovery is not an inductive generalization, but his discussion does not uncover a mode of inference from observational data to theory. Yet his discussion adds a new requirement for an adequate account of induction in theoretical inference.

(5) Even the "same" terms are new in the sense that they are given an extended use in the theory—a use which gives new inference techniques.

There is another widely recognized argument which suggests that theory formation cannot be based on inductive generalizations from data. The starting point of this argument is the recognition that there is an important sense in which observation presupposes theory. There are many clear discussions of this point;[12] in the following sketch, I shall start with Hanson's remarks on observations. Hanson maintained that two scientists working from radically different theoretical standpoints do not "see the same thing" and interpret what they see in different manners—each according to his respective theoretical context. They may have the same retinal image, or the same "sense-datum experience," but these experiences of seeing already involve interpretation: "Theories and interpretations are 'there' in the seeing from the outset."[13] Hence in coming to see something differently, it is not a mere question of reinterpretation of what one sees. Rather a "gestalt-switch" in theoretical understanding must come before the seeing in a different manner.[14] In summary, Hanson is insisting that "observation of x is shaped by prior knowledge of x,"[15] that is to say, it is knowledge as to the behavior of x which is specified by a theory which in an important sense determines the observation of x as x.[16]

Kuhn agrees with Hanson's point that all observation is theory-laden and that changes in observation involve gestalt-switches in theory. "What a man sees depends both upon what he looks at and also upon what his previous visual-conceptual experience has taught him to see. In the absence of such training there can only be, in William James' phrase, "a boomin' buzzin' confusion'."[17] Kuhn uses the thesis of the theory-ladenness of observations to extend the argument against induction from observation to theory: without an established theory one cannot distinguish relevant from irrelevant observations. Hence there is no simple generalization from data to theory because theory is presupposed in the collection of relevant data.[18]

Feyerabend has developed the argument along slightly different lines. If one starts from the thesis of the theory-ladenness of observation, it is clear that new theories cannot be induced from observations for the following reason—all the observations will support the accepted theory. New theories can arise only with the overthrow of accepted ones, and such an overthrow can come about only with the existence of competing theories which determine observations which would not have been made under the accepted theory and which conflict with the accepted theory.[19] We have already seen how Feyerabend has turned this argument into a defense of the necessity of "metaphysics" for science, where metaphysical theories are conceived as alternatives to accepted theories. In general his argument suggests that scientific method should be counter-inductive in a wide sense. The scientific enterprise should consist of proposing theories counter to the available observations, not induced from them.[20]

On the whole, then, historical relativists have maintained that theory is prior to observation and that this thesis entails that in theory formation there is no simple inductive move from data to theory. Their argument suggests a further criterion which must be met by any adequate account of the role of induction in theory formation.

(6) Induction is not in its essence generalization from particular to general.

21. "Valid inductive inference"

The contemporary discussion of the role of induction which best takes account of (1)-(6) is that of Mary Hesse. She explicitly accepts (6) in distinguishing the "problem of the *validation* of induction which Hume found to be insoluble" and the problem of the "*explication* of the concept of 'valid induction'."[21] Hesse explains what she means by an explication of "valid induction":

> I shall assume that the aim of an explication of 'valid induction' is to find a numerical or comparative function $c(h,e)$—the 'confirmation of hypothesis h given evidence e'—which is a syntactic function of the statements h and e. and which has a high or comparatively high value in those cases where normally accepted or intuitive inductive methods would direct us to accept hypothesis h on evidence e, at least in comparison with other hypotheses having lower c-value.[22]

In a less technical sense she means the explication of "inductive inferences of a kind generally regarded as justifiable"—inductive inferences to theories and to predictions.[23]

Hesse's explication of "valid induction" is developed from criticisms of attempts to develop the logic of confirmation. In an early work Hempel suggested "conditions of adequacy for any definition of confirmation." These included the following:

C_1: Special Consequence Condition: An observational report that confirms a theory confirms every logical consequence of the theory.

C_2: Converse Consequence Condition: An observational report that is entailed by a theory confirms the theory.[24]

Hesse argues that a problem arises if both C_1 and C_2 are accepted. It arises for the special case when a theory t is equivalent to the conjunction of two sets of observational reports, e_1 and e_2. In this case t entails e_1 and e_2. Hence by C_2, e_1 confirms t; by C_1, e_1 confirms e_2. However the latter conclusion is unacceptable because e_2 may be unrelated to e_1. "If t is produced just by arbitrarily conjoining any other statement e_2 to e_1, we should certainly not want a confirmation theory in general to allow e_1 to confirm e_2. Some further conditions must be imposed upon admissible e_1 and e_2 and either C_1 or C_2 must be modified."[25]

In view of this difficulty Hempel first rejected C_2 but later rejected C_1 in favor of C_2. The consequences of rejecting C_1 were made clear by H. Putnam's critique of Carnap's theory of confirmation.[26] If a theory t entails e_1 and e_2, e_1 is *not* more probable in virtue of the common deducibility of e_1 and e_2 from t than on the basis of e_1 alone. It would seem, then, that "valid inductive inferences" are from particulars to particulars; theories are "redundant."[27]

On the other hand this conclusion seems to run counter to the scientist's notion of "valid induction." On the whole e_2 is considered to be better confirmed when there is theoretical evidence for it than when such evidence is lacking.[28] In her discussions Hesse cites Putnam's example of the prediction of the explosion of the first atomic bomb.[29] From e_1 (physical and chemical evidence) the prediction e_2 (the explosion) was warranted to the scientist's mind because of the mediation of nuclear theory. It would seem, then, that a possible construal of "valid induction" (inferences to predictions and theories scientists find to be good inductions) might be the following inference pattern.

(1)

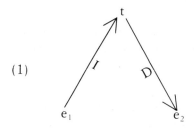

where e_1 represents initial evidence; e_2 represents predictions; $\longrightarrow$I represents an inductive inference from e_1 to a theory t; $\longrightarrow$D represents a deductive inference from theory t to predictions; and t $\longrightarrow$D $e_1 \cdot e_1$.

Hesse argues, however, that inference pattern (1) is inadequate, because it suggests that e_2 is more probable in virtue of its relation to e_1 via t than on the basis of e_1 alone. Yet this is not the case. "No probabilistic confirmation theory of any type yet developed will allow us to infer with greater than prior confirmation from e_1 to e_2 *merely in virtue of the fact that both are deductive consequences of some theory.*"[30] Hesse's point is that t does not add to the probability of e_2 because the probability of t is derived from e_1 and e_2. "Theories cannot be pulled up by their own boot straps, but only by support from external models."[31] In general the inference from e_1 to e_2 is not justified unless there is a "probabilistic dependence" between e_1 and e_2 "independent" of their deducibility from t.[32]

The probabilistic relation which suffices to justify the inference from e_1 to e_2 which Hesse takes to be the clue to an adequate inference pattern is that of analogy. Her schematic inference pattern is the following:[33]

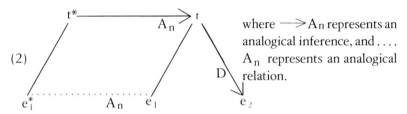

(2)

where $\longrightarrow A_n$ represents an analogical inference, and . . . . A_n represents an analogical relation.

Here the inductive inference involved is an analogical one from t^* to t based upon an analogy between e_1^* and e_1; t deductively entails e_2. There is no questionable generalization from evidence to theory. The inference, rather, is from particulars to particulars. But theories are not redundant. In Hesse's view theories are not to be conceived as arranged in layers such that higher levels are generalizations from lower ones and allow predictions on the lower levels to be deduced. However theories do have a role to play. Her "tentative suggestion" is that "the function of the theory is the indication and systematic extraction (or abstraction) of analogies between a number of empirical systems."[34] Hence her view is able to explicate inferences of a kind scientists find justifiable.

These notions constitute an elaboration of Hesse's view that theoretical inference always takes place by way of a model or analogy for which laws are already known.[35]

This brief discussion suffices to show that Hesse's account meets the requirements (1)-(6). New terms are accounted for because t is developed by analogy from t^*. The analogical inference from t^* to t is not mechanical. Imagination is required in developing t on the model of t^*. The "same" terms have an extended use in t and provide "new inferring techniques"—deductions to e_2. The induction to t is not a generalization from particular to general; the role of prior theory is fully accounted for. It is an inductive inference pattern and not a general principle of induction that is being explicated.

It is at this point that the organic philosophy has a contribution to make. The "valid inductive inference" pattern has been explicated, but has it been justified? I think not. In order to make good this claim I shall compare Hesse's view with passages from Whitehead's writings about induction. Most of these passages contain the term "environment." It is my contention that the concepts of organism and environment and the metaphysical doctrines they entail are required for the justification of a "valid inductive inference" pattern.

22. Environment and the justification of "valid inductive inference"

I wish to suggest that Whitehead held a theory about the "explication of the concept of 'valid induction'" quite similar to (2). The language is strikingly different because he was writing about generic "valid inductions" rather than what has come to be a technical problem in the logic of confirmation. Whitehead clearly maintained the basis of "valid inductions" to be analogy.

> Thus, according to the philosophy of organism, inductive reasoning gains its validity by reason of a suppressed premise. This tacit presupposition is that the particular future which is the logical subject of the judgment, inductively justified, shall include actualities which have a close analogy to some contemporary subject enjoying assigned experience. . . . It is also presumed that this future is derived from the present by a continuity of inheritance in which this condition is maintained. There is thus the presupposition of the maintenance of the general social environment (PR 310).

> An inductive argument always includes an hypothesis, namely, that the environment which is the subject matter considered contains a society of actual occasions analogous to the society in the present. But analogous societies require analogous data for their several occasions; and analogous data can be provided only by the objectifications provided by analogous environments. But the laws of nature are derived from the characters of the societies dominating the environment. Thus the laws of nature dominating the environment in question have some analogy to the laws of nature dominating the immediate environment (PR 312).

> Thus the basis of all probability and induction is the fact of analogy between an environment presupposed and an environment directly experienced (PR 314).

Whitehead includes in this discussion a passage from SMW which he calls a "summary" of the first passage quoted above.

> You will observe that I do not hold induction to be in its essence the derivation of general laws. It is the derivation of some characteristics of a particular future from the known characteristics of a particular past. The wider assumption of

general laws holding for all cognizable occasions appears a very unsafe addendum to attach to this limited knowledge (PR 310).

These passages suffice to show a prima facie closeness of Whitehead's position to Hesse's. An inference pattern can be abstracted from these passages with the same form as (2).

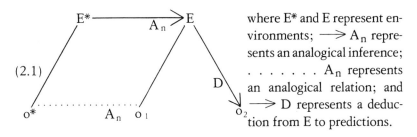

(2.1)

where E* and E represent environments; $\longrightarrow A_n$ represents an analogical inference; . . . . . . A_n represents an analogical relation; and $\longrightarrow D$ represents a deduction from E to predictions.

There is an analogical inference from environment E* to environment E based on an analogical relation between the organisms o* and o of the respective environments. Since laws of nature are abstractions from an environmental order, one can deduce predictions as to the behavior and properties of the organisms o_2; these organisms will conform to the laws expressing the dominant order of environment E.

However the reference to environment suggests that more is being assumed in inference pattern (2.1) than is explicit in Hesse's inference pattern (2). In order to make this assumption explicit, it will be necessary to apply the concept of environment to (2.1).

An inductive inference (such as that involved in theory formation) shifts reference from one environment (E*) to another (E). Each environment is necessary for the existence of its organisms. The organisms of E (o_1) cannot exist without the order provided by E and those of E* (o*) cannot exist without the environmental order of E*. It is because of this condition for the existence of organisms that analogy between the organisms of the two environments warrants an inference to be made as to the analogical relationship between the two environments. Further, since laws of nature are a statement of dominant environmental order, there is a context for inferring predictions about the behavior of other organisms in the environment to which reference has been shifted—organisms not explicitly considered in the original analogies.

101

We can now see how the doctrine of internal relations is involved, for Whitehead, in a "valid inductive inference." The relationship between any organism and its environment is an internal one, and the inductive inference is "valid" ultimately in virtue of this internal relation between organism and environment.[36] A passage earlier cited is relevant here:

> Survival requires order, and to propose survival, apart from the type of order which that type of survival requires is a contradiction. It is at this point that the organic philosophy differs from any form of Cartesian 'substance-philosophy.' For if a substance requires nothing but itself in order to exist, its survival can tell no tale as to the survival of order in its environment. Thus no conclusion can be drawn respecting the external relationships of the surviving substance to its future environment. For the organic philosophy, anticipations as to the future of a piece of rock presuppose an environment with the type of order which that piece of rock requires. Thus the completely unknown environment never enters into an inductive judgment (PR 311-12).

In brief the internal relationship between an organism and its environment is a necessary condition for a "valid inductive inference." It is not, however, a sufficient condition. I think Whitehead recognized this in bringing up the point that analogy leaves a "margin of uncertainty."

> Now the notions of 'analogy' and of 'dominance' both leave a margin of uncertainty. We can ask, How far analogous? and How far dominant? If there were exact analogy, and complete dominance, there would be a mixture of certainty as to the general conditions and of complete ignorance as to specific details. But such a description does not apply either to our knowledge of the immediate present, or of the past, or to our inductive knowledge of the future. Our conscious experience involves a baffling mixture of certainty, ignorance, and probability (PR 312-13).

The "valid inductive inference" pattern (2.1)—abstracted from the passages prior to this passage—suggests that Whitehead's meaning was simply that *if* there is analogy, a further condition for making the inference is still required, *viz.,* the internal relationships between organisms and environments. But this is not sufficient. It still remains to determine whether or not there is sufficient positive analogy. At this point Whitehead adds further assumptions—a lower limit to the relevance of the environment and a lower limit to the data for prehensions. These assumptions have been shown to amount to the Keynesian principle of the limitation of independent variety.[37] These additional assumptions are necessary for determining whether or not there is sufficient similarity to warrant the inference from one environment to another. But the inference from one environment to another is also grounded in the metaphysical doctrine of internal relations, and this grounding is the prior one. The denial of the necessity of the doctrine of internal relations leaves one with Hume's problem, which is indeed insoluble:

> The question, as to what will happen to an unspecified entity in an unspecified environment, has no answer (PR 312).

The presupposition of internal relations is not sufficient to specify the organism. But in virtue of the doctrine of internal relations, if the organism is specified, so are some aspects of its environment.

Let us now return to assess the resemblance of the inference patterns (2) and (2.1). In both patterns the induction is essentially "from particular to particular" and is founded on analogy—the analogy between the organisms constituting the evidence and that between systematizations of order relevant to those organisms (theories or environments). Both are claiming that an analogy between the two sets of evidence warrants an analogy between the two systems of order bound up with the respective evidence; and the system of order to which the inference is made deductively entails certain predictions. That is, an analogy between e_1^* (o_1^*) and e_1 (o_1), and an analogical inference from t^* (E^*) to t (E), and the fact that $t \longrightarrow e_2 (E \longrightarrow o_2)$ warrants the conclusion e_2 (o_2) with higher than prior confirmation. Both insist that theoretical inference takes place by way of a model whose order is already known (theory or environment); t^* (E^*) is a model for the elucidation of t (E).

However the reference to environment in (2.1) involves the metaphysical doctrine of internal relations, whereas in (2) no claim is made about metaphysical doctrines of any kind. Indeed Hesse eschews metaphysical justifications of induction.[38] But in what sense can this be done? Is inference pattern (2) a "valid inductive inference" if the doctrine of internal relations is not an implicit necessary condition? I do not think that it is. The Whiteheadian argument seems quite general; it is about generic valid inductions. Let us reconsider this argument in face of the claim that such postulates as the Keynesian principle of limitation of independent variety constitute adequate grounding for "valid inductive inference."

The Whiteheadian argument, as we have seen, is that "valid inductive inference" requires that the existence of any organism (and thereby the

103

behavior and properties of that organism) be bound up with an environmental order. This is an assertion of internal relatedness. The organisms of an environment contribute to the environmental order and, at the same time, the organisms cannot exist without that environmental order. The alternative to recognizing the internal relatedness of organism and environment is to assert that an organism does not require a particular environmental order to exist. In this case it seems quite clear that inference pattern (2) is not a "valid inductive inference" because the analogies between organisms cannot be a ground for analogies between systems of order. Organisms could exist under any alternative orders and inductive inference, it seems, could *never* be justified.

The Keynesian argument, however, seems to be at odds with the Whiteheadian one. Keynes maintains that a "valid inductive inference" requires that the "universe of phenomena . . . present those peculiar characteristics of atomism and limited variety which appear more and more clearly as the ultimate result to which material science is tending."[39] These two assumptions are not "formally equivalent" but are tantamount to the same thing.[40] Atomic uniformity is a thesis about the relationship of parts to complexes into which they enter (or organize).[41] The limitation of independent variety is an assumption to insure that the number of properties relevant to the behavior of any object is not infinite.[42] This assumption guarantees that the probability of finding a particular set of properties in unobserved cases when they have already been observed together will be increased.[43]

Keynes' argument as to why these two assumptions are required for "valid inductive inference" is crucial for resolving the conflict about the role of the doctrine of internal relations. Consider the following two passages.

> Yet there might well be quite different laws for wholes of different degrees of complexity, and laws of connection between complexes which could not be stated in terms of laws connecting individual parts. In this case natural law would be organic, and not, as it is generally supposed, atomic. If every configuration of the universe were subject to a separate and independent law, or if very small differences between bodies—in their shape and size, for instance, —led to their obeying quite different laws, predictions would be impossible and the inductive method useless. Yet nature might still be uniform, causation sovereign, and laws timeless and absolute.
>
> The scientist wishes, in fact, to assume that the occurrence of a phenomenon

which has appeared as part of a more complex phenomenon, may be *some* reason for expecting it to be associated on another occasion with part of the same complex. Yet if different wholes were subject to different laws *qua* wholes and not simply on account of and in proportion to the differences of their parts, knowledge of a part could not lead, it would seem, even to presumptive or probable knowledge as to its association with other parts. Given, on the other hand, a number of legally atomic events and the laws connecting them, it would be possible to deduce their effects *pro tanto* without an exhaustive knowledge of all the coexisting circumstances.[44]

If the fundamental laws of connection changed altogether with variations, for instance, in the shape or size of bodies, or if the laws governing the behavior of a complex had no relation whatever to the laws governing the behavior of its parts when belonging to other complexes, there could hardly be a limitation of independent variety in the sense in which this has been defined. And, on the other hand, a limitation of independent variety seems necessarily to carry with it some degree of atomic uniformity. The underlying conception as to the character of the System of Nature is in each case the same.[45]

In these passages Keynes is maintaining that one must make an assumption to guarantee the limitation of independent variety. If laws for complexes were not expressible in terms of laws governing the parts of complexes, then different complexes into which the same parts enter could be governed by quite different laws (indeed—incompatible ones). That is, knowledge of the behavior of parts in one complex could never warrant knowledge of the behavior of the same parts in another complex. Hence predictions would not be possible, and no explication could be given of "valid inductive inference." What is required, then, is that the laws governing the behavior of parts in one complex be related to laws governing those parts in other complexes.

It seems to me that the Keynesian necessary condition for the limitation of independent variety is an affirmation of the Whiteheadian claim that "survival requires order."

It may seem as if Keynes is maintaining a materialistic mechanism with respect to the relationship of parts and complexes which contradicts the organic conception. However this is not the case. Both Whitehead and Keynes are maintaining the following: If $(a_1, \ldots, a_n)$ organize complex C^* and $(a_1, \ldots, a_r)$ organize complex C, then the laws governing a_1 must include a description of the behavior of a_1 in both C^* and C—behavior which we *empirically* know is rarely the same. But this amounts to saying that what a_1 *is* depends upon the orders which it forms: a complete decription of a_1 cannot be given without reference to its potential to behave differently in different complexes. Clearly this constitutes a rejection of what Whitehead terms the "Cartesian 'substance-philosophy'." Such a rejection is necessary if predictions are to be made and "valid inductions" justified. To repeat: "For if a substance requires nothing but itself in order to exist, its survival can tell no tale as to the survival of order in its environment. Thus no conclusion can be drawn respecting the external relationships of the surviving substance to its future environment" (PR 311).

Thus it seems that any explication of "valid inductive inference" requires as a necessary condition the metaphysical doctrine of internal relations. This doctrine is a necessary condition for the limitation of independent variety, which is, in turn, a necessary condition for "valid inductive inference" to predictions and to theories.

In summary, the organic philosophy finds a role for induction in theoretical inference which satisfies the criteria (1)-(6). Other views, for example Hesse's, which seem to satisfy (1)-(6), omit the necessary metaphysical presupposition of internal relations which is entailed in the organic concepts of organism and environment. It is clear that the doctrine of internal relations is a necessary condition for justifying "valid inductive inference" patterns because the recognized necessary conditions for such patterns are grounded in this metaphysical doctrine.

IX. Explanation

23. The orthodox empiricist models of explanation

The orthodox empiricist view of explanation insists upon the ideal of deductive form.

> Ever since Aristotle analyzed the structure of what he believed to be the ideal of science, the view that scientific explanations must always be rendered in the form of a logical deduction has had wide acceptance. Although the universality of the deductive pattern may be open to question, even when the pattern is projected as an ideal, it is hardly disputable that many explanations in the sciences —and indeed the most comprehensive and impressive systems of explanation —are of this form. Moreover, many explanations that ostensibly fail to realize this form can be shown to exemplify it, when the assumptions that are taken for granted in the explanations are made explicit; and such cases may count not as exceptions to the deductive model, but as illustrations of the frequent use of enthymematic arguments. [1]

One of the most rigorous accounts of this deductive model is that of Hempel and Oppenheim.[2] Their schema for a deductive explanation is as follows:[3]

$$
\text{Logical deduction}
\left[
\begin{array}{l}
\left\{
\begin{array}{ll}
C_1, C_2, \ldots, C_k & \text{Statements of antecedent} \\
& \text{conditions} \\
\\
L_1, L_2, \ldots, L_r & \text{General laws}
\end{array}
\right. \\
\hline
\longrightarrow E \quad\quad \text{Description of the empiri-} \\
\text{cal phenomenon to be} \\
\text{explained}
\end{array}
\right.
$$

Explanans

Explanandum

Hempel and Oppenheim list three logical conditions of adequacy for the explanation in this form—(R_1)-(R_3)—and one empirical condition of adequacy—(R_4).[4]

(R_1) The explanans deductively entails the explanandum.
(R_2) The explanans contains (at least) one universal law which is actually used in the deduction.
(R_3) The explanans has empirical import.
(R_4) The statements of the explanans have not been falsified.

In addition it is claimed that prediction has the same logical structure as explanation.[5] That is, the above schema applies equally to explanation and to prediction.

In Hempel's later works, e.g., *Philosophy of Natural Science* and "Deductive-Nomological vs. Statistical Explanation," the deductive pattern of explanation is unchanged.[6] However he maintains that all explanations in science are not of deductive form.[7] In particular there are explanation patterns (say, in genetics, quantum mechanics, and sociology)[8] which differ from the deductive pattern in that (1) the laws of the explanans are not universal but statistical in character, (2) the explanandum is a description of an empirical phenomenon belonging to the class described by the statistical law, and (3) the relationship between explanans and explanandum is not deductive. Hempel gives the following schemata:[9]

Explanans {
  The probability that O is an R is close to 1
  i is a case of R
}

_____ [makes highly probable]
_____
  i is a case of O   } Explanandum

or

Explanans {
  The probability that O is an R
  i is a case of R
}

_____ [r]
_____
  i is a case of O   } Explanandum

Other patterns of scientific explanation are distinguished from these two basic patterns by the formalists. Hempel cites "motivational" and "teleological" explanations,[10] and Nagel "teleological" and "genetic" explanations.[11] These two patterns are generally distinguished for explanations in biology and the social sciences (including history).

Although patterns of explanation are distinguished in addition to the deductive pattern, the deductive pattern is considered by formalists to be the ideal of explanation and other patterns of explanation to be problematic and to be candidates for modification to patterns that approximate the deductive one as closely as possible.

24. Explanation as an activity of scientists

Historical relativists are in agreement that the ideal of deductive explanation is to be rejected because it distorts an understanding of the process of conceptual change. The grounds for the rejection are the same as those for the rejection of induction in theory formation, *viz.,* theoretical determination of observational terms.

The deductive pattern of explanation sets up a sharp distinction between theoretical and observational language. This distinction puts clear demands on an explanation which is of deductive form. If the explanandum consists of observation statements, correspondence rules are required to connect the theoretical meaning of the explanans with the observational meaning of the explanandum. There are immense difficulties with respect to how the correspondence rules are to be conceived. These difficulties have been discussed at length, by formalists themselves,[12] and by opponents of the formalist view.[13] These discussions need not concern us here. It suffices to note that these rules are problematic. If, on the other hand, the explanandum consists of theoretical statements (more general theories explaining less general theories), it must be assumed that the meaning of the "same" terms appearing in the theories does not vary. A deduction of explanandum from explanans can be carried out only if these demands are met.

It is clear that these demands for an explanation conflict with the thesis of the theory-ladenness of observational meaning. This thesis entails that there is no sharp distinction between observational and theoretical language, at least in the sense that the formalists claim, and that the "same" terms in different theories do not necessarily mean the same thing.

109

It is clear also that historical relativists can use this conflict between deduction and theory-ladenness to maintain that the deductive model of explanation stands in the way of theoretical advance. Feyeraband's version of the argument is as follows: the deductive model presupposes two conditions which must be rejected. These are the "consistency condition," which requires that any new theory introduced in a particular field of science be logically compatible with the accepted theories in that field, and the "condition of meaning invariance," which requires that the meaning of terms remain invariant in successive theories.[14] These conditions are necessary for an explanation of deductive form, yet they hamper theoretical advance for reasons considered in section 20. They guarantee the continued acceptance of established theories. Observations which might potentially falsify the accepted theory are not recognized; hence any new theory is eliminated, not because it disagrees with observations, but because it disagrees with established theories.

The difficulties which the deductive model of explanation poses for conceptual change have led to a wide consensus among historical relativists with respect to a view of explanation. "We have to conclude . . . that a formal and 'objective' account of explanation cannot be given."[15] "The heart of recent arguments about conceptual change in science is the insight that no single ideal of 'explanation', or rational justification —such as Plato and Descartes found in formal geometry—is applicable universally in all sciences at all times."[16]

The understanding of explanation which is being rejected is the formalist notion that explanation can be reduced to deduction; instead it is being insisted that explanations can be given in many modes, deductive argumentation being merely one of these modes. Toulmin has described this view as a reversal of the roles of "argument" and "activity" in explanation.[17] He maintains that "activity of explaining" is the generic term and that giving arguments is one species of this activity; other species of explanatory activity include "the drawing of graphs or ray-diagrams, the construction of intellectual models, or the programming of computers."[18] These activities are not deductive proofs but "explantory procedures."

A procedural account of explanation is to be understood in terms of modes of behavior. The general procedures involve more than formal arguments, and explanation requires both the employment of the general procedures and the recognition of the scope of the procedure.[20]

110

The procedures and their scope in any given field are determined by a paradigm[21] for that field. The notion of paradigm and paradigm change will be the main topic of Chapter X.

An implication of the procedural account of explanation is that, in the fundamental sense, it is scientists who explain; theories explain only in a derivative sense. "Nor can any abstract general theory ever in and by itself, 'explain' or 'represent' natural phenomena; rather it is scientists who employ this theory—in the particular manner they do, in the specific cases they do, and with the degree of success they do—to represent, and so explain, the properties of behaviour of independently identified classes of system or object."[22]

In summary, the historical relativist view of explanation is that any particular explanation in science may be unique. To understand explanation one must analyze particular examples of explanation to see what explanatory procedures the scientist used. It is not to be expected that the same procedures will be involved in every explanation nor that one procedure will dominate in a class of explanations.

25. Organism and explanation—metaphysical and scientific

The organic philosophy of science as thus far developed seems to raise difficulties for fitting explanation to any of the orthodox empiricist models. In the first place it seems that, in the organic view, the deductive ideal of explanation must be ruled out. The deductive pattern of explanation requires at least one universal law to be included in the explanans; and, as we have seen, there are no universal laws in the organic view—all laws are statistical in character. In addition although the organic account of theoretical inference (sections 21 and 22) gives a role to deduction in prediction, the role is a minor one and depends upon an inductive analogical inference.

Second, since laws in the organic view are statistical in character, it might seem as if the probabilistic model is the paradigm of explanation. However all explanation cannot be reduced to particular events of an environment. There are layers of environmental order, and laws are the dominant orders abstracted from the more general environments.

The explanation of laws of less general environments by more general laws must be accounted for. The probabilistic model is inadequate for doing this because the explanandum is a description of a particular event. Further, the "valid inductive inference" pattern accepted by the organic view is not adequately described by the simple relation of "makes highly probable" or "r" in the relation of explanans and explanandum in the probabilistic model.

Third, complications arise also with the teleological and genetic models of explanation. The organic view is a radical evolutionary view. All levels of organization in nature—electrons and protons as well as biological species—evolve; laws of nature are capable of evolving. Hence there is a sense in which ultimate explanation must be genetic. Further, since the organic notion of genetic explanation involves implicit reference to purpose (see, e.g., FR, 26f and SMW 156-58), genetic explanation is not essentially separable from functional-teleological explanation. Hence it seems impossible that the organic view be conceived in terms of any of the general patterns of scientific explanation distinguished by the formalists.

The historical relativist construal of explanation as an activity of scientists is also unacceptable for the organic view. Whitehead clearly rejected the notion that scientific explanation could be conceived in terms of the activity of scientists (FR 54-55). In addition there is no doctrine in the philosophy of organism which suggests that one argument pattern cannot be involved in all explanation (although, as we have seen, the deductive pattern cannot be the one so involved). Indeed the doctrine of the immanence of laws suggests that there is a fundamental sense in which the theories into which these laws are incorporated explain, independently of the activity of scientists.

The impossibility of conceiving explanation in the organic view in terms of both of these traditions requires that the organic view of metaphysical explanation be developed and compared with a very general view of organic explanation in science.

In Whitehead's view, explanation in the generic sense is metaphysical; scientific explanation is a species of this generic sense.

> The cosmological scheme should present the genus, for which the special schemes of the sciences are the species (FR 76).

The outcome of both the metaphysical and the scientific enterprise is the same, *viz.,* the understanding of facts (and less general principles) in terms of general principles (more general principles). Whitehead describes the "full scientific mentality" as holding "that all things great and small are conceivable as exemplifications of general principles which reign throughout the natural order" (SMW 7). In other passages he links science and philosophy together. Science and philosophy

> are both concerned with the understanding of individual facts as illustrations of general principles. The principles are understood in the abstract and the facts are understood in respect to their embodiment of the principles (AI 179).

> The first step in science and philosophy has been taken when it is grasped that every routine exemplifies a principle which is capable of statement in abstrac-·tion from its particular exemplifications (AI 180-81).

This outcome is achieved by the method referred to as "generalization." That is, the method of explanation is that of "generalization." "Generalization" is the discovery of generic principles from a study of a species of facts (or lower-level principles).

> The first requisite is to proceed by the method of generalization so that certainly there is some application; and the test of some success is application beyond the immediate origin. In other words, some synoptic vision has been gained.

> In this description of philosophic method, the term 'philosophic generalization' has meant 'the utilization of specific notions, applying to a restricted group of facts, for the divination of the generic notions which apply to all facts' (PR 8).

Although this passage refers to "philosophical generalization," Whitehead maintains that the natural sciences use this method as well (PR 8).

Whitehead also describes the method of science and philosophy as a logic of discovery.

> The Greeks invented logic in the broadest sense of that term—the logic of discovery. The Greek logic as finally perfected by the experience of centuries provides a set of criteria to which the content of a belief should be subjected. These are:
>   (i) Conformity to intuitive experience:
>   (ii) Clarity of the propositional content:
>   (iii) Internal Logical consistency:
>   (iv) External Logical consistency:
>   (v) Status of a *Logical* scheme with,
>   (a) widespread conformity to experience,
>   (b) no discordance with experience,
>   (c) coherence among its categorical notions,
>   (d) methodological consequences. . . .

> The whole point of the fifth criterion is that the scheme produces a greater understanding of the world, including the better definition of ideas and the more direct analysis of immediate fact. A single proposition rests upon vague apprehensions: whereas a scheme of ideas provides its own measure of definiteness by the mutual relatedness of its own categoreal methods.
>
> It is by their emphasis on schemes of thought that the Greeks founded the various branches of science, which have remade civilization. A proposition which falls within a scientific scheme is accepted with surprisingly slight direct verification (FR 67-70).

These passages suffice to make it clear that there is no difference in kind between philosophical and scientific method in explanation.

Wherein lies the difference in science and philosophy? There can be no doubt that Whitehead maintained the difference to lie in the degree of generality of the generic concepts attained by the "generalization" in each enterprise.

> The field of a special science is confined to one genus of facts, in the sense that no statements are made respecting facts which lie outside that genus. . . .
>
> The study of philosophy is a voyage towards the larger generalities (PR 14).

In FR Whitehead distinguishes two aspects of Reason—the "Reason of Plato" which seeks "a complete understanding" and the "Reason of Ulysses" which seeks "an immediate method of action" (FR 11).

> Two aspects of the function of Reason have been discriminated. In one aspect, the function of Reason was practical. To its operation the piecemeal discovery and clarification of methodology is due. In this way it not only elaborates the methodology, but also lifts into conscious experience the detailed operations possible within limits of that method. In this respect, Reason is the enlightenment of purpose; within limits, it renders purpose effective. Also when it has rendered purpose effective, it has fulfilled its function and lulls itself with self-satisfaction. It has finished its task. This aspect of the operations of Reason was connected with the legend of Ulysses.
>
> The other aspect of the function of Reason was connected with the life-work of Plato. In this function Reason is enthroned above the practical tasks of the world. It is not concerned with keeping alive. It seeks with disinterested curiosity an understanding of the world. Naught that happens is alien to it. It is driven forward by the ultimate faith that all particular fact is understandable as illustrating the general .principles of its own nature and of its status among other particular facts. It fulfils its function when understanding has been gained. Its sole satisfaction is that experience has been understood (FR 37-38).

Can this method of "generalization," by which science and philosophy explain, be more specifically characterized? One can begin such a specification by a negative characterization. This method is *not* in its essence *deductive.*

> Philosophy has been haunted by the unfortunate notion that its method is dogmatically to indicate premises which are severally clear, distinct, and certain; and to erect upon those premises a deductive system of thought.
>
> But the accurate expression of the final generalities is the goal of discussion and not its origin. Philosophy has been misled by the example of mathematics (PR 11-12).
>
> The primary method of mathematics is deduction; the primary method of philosophy is descriptive generalization. Under the influence of mathematics, deduction has been foisted onto philosophy as its standard method, instead of taking its true place as an essential auxiliary mode of verification whereby to test the scope of generalities (PR 15-16).
>
> Philosophy is the search for premises. It is not deduction. Such deductions as occur are for the purpose of testing the starting-points by the evidence of the conclusions (MT 143).

These passages confirm the earlier considerations with regard to the impossibility of conceiving the ideal of organic explanation in terms of the deductive model. The essence of explanation is not deductive; the explanandum is not explained by virtue of being deductively derived from the explanans. The role of deduction is an "auxiliary" one bound up with confirmation. It is clear that these passages are in complete accord with the notion of "valid inductive inference" elaborated in section 21. In this inference pattern the deductive inference is to predictions which test the proposed dominant order of an environment elaborated analogically, not deductively, from the model of another environmental order.

Any attempt to positively characterize the method of explanation is hampered by Whitehead's occasional references to the impossibility of such a characterization. He uses such terms as "self-evidence" and "direct insight" in describing this method. Indeed he even maintains that philosophy is "untrammelled by method":

> The speculative Reason is in its essence untrammelled by method. Its function is to pierce into the general reasons beyond limited reasons, to understand all methods as coordinated in a nature of things only to be grasped by transcending all method (FR 65).

But Whitehead need not be maintaining that there is no positive char-

115

acterization of this method. His point is, rather, that "philosophical generalization" transcends particular methodologies. Similarly we have seen that "scientific generalization" discovers methodology ("In one aspect, the function of Reason was practical. To its operation that piecemeal *discovery* and clarification of methodologies is due [italics mine]"). The implication is that the generalized explanatory notions of scientific and philosophical theory are prior to methodology. Whitehead expresses this as "theory dictates method":

> So far as concerns methodology, the general issue of the discussion will be that theory dictates method, and that any particular method is only applicable to theories of one correlate species. An analogous conclusion holds for the technical terms. This close relation of theory to method partly arises from the fact that the relevance of evidence depends on the theory which is dominating the discussion. This fact is the reason why dominant theories are also termed 'working hypotheses' (AI 283).

This passage is an important one, for it not only suggests the priority of theory to method (and hence rules out any mechanical conception of "scientific generalization"—inductive or deductive), but also suggests that an analogous connection be made between a theory and its technical terms as the historical relativists have maintained. Whitehead is rejecting the condition of meaning invariance. Other passages in his writings explicitly reject the notion of meaning invariance. For example:[23]

> Mankind found itself in possession of certain concepts respecting nature—for example, the concept of fairly permanent material bodies—and proceeded to determine laws which related the corresponding precepts in nature. But the formulation of laws changed the concepts—sometimes gently by an added precision, sometimes violently. At first this process was not much noticed, or at least was felt to be process curbed within narrow bounds, not touching fundamental ideas. At the stage where we are now, the formulation of the concepts can be seen to be as important as the formulation of the empirical laws connecting the events in the universe as thus conceived by us: for example, the concepts of life, of heredity, of a material body, of a molecule, of an atom, of an electron, of energy, of space, of time, of quantity, and of number.

The topic of meaning invariance will be given careful consideration in Chapter X. For the present discussion it suffices to point out that explanation, for Whitehead, requires a rejection of this thesis. Part of the positive characterization of "philosophical" and "scientific generalization" involves extension in the meaning of the concepts which describe

116

the explanandum.

> Our understanding outruns the ordinary usages of words. Philosophy is akin to poetry. Philosophy is the endeavor to find a conventional phraseology for the vivid suggestiveness of the poet. . . (MT 68-69).

> Language is incomplete and fragmentary, and merely registers a stage in the average advance beyond ape-mentality. But all men enjoy flashes of insight beyond meanings already stabilized in etymology and grammar. Hence the role of literature, the role of the special sciences, and the role of philosophy: — in their various ways engaged in finding linguistic expressions for meanings as yet unexpressed (AI 291).

What is the key to "finding linguistic expressions for meanings as yet unexpressed?" I suggest that Whitehead conceived the key to be in the notion of metaphor.

> Philosophers can never hope finally to formulate these metaphysical first principles. Weakness of insight and deficiencies of language stand in the way inexorably. Words and phrases must be stretched toward a generality foreign to their ordinary usage; and however such elements of language be stabilized as technicalities, they remain metaphors mutely appealing for the imaginative leap (PR 6).

> Progress in truth—truth of science and truth of religion—is mainly a progress in the framing of concepts, in discarding artificial abstractions or partial metaphors, and in evolving notions which strike more deeply into the root of reality (RM 127).

The use of metaphor in explanation is a topic which has been developed in contemporary philosophy of science.[24] The next section will summarize one such discussion. The concluding section of this chapter will relate the metaphorical view to the concept of environment.

26. Metaphor, analogy, and explanation

The metaphorical view of explanation which I wish to consider is that of Mary Hesse.[25] Her view is a development of the "interaction view" of metaphor suggested by Max Black.[26] In this view there are two sets of statements, one constituting a literal description of the explanandum, the other constituting a literal description of the explanans. Language is used metaphorically, and not literally, when words ordinarily used in the literal description of the explanans are transferred to the explanandum.[27] Such a use of language is not to be thought of as a comparison. That is, it is not posssible to replace the metaphor "by an explicit, literal statement of the similarities between" the explanandum and explanans.[28] It is not a comparison for two reasons. First, the fruitfulness of the explanans is bound up with the fact that the extent of the comparison is unknown. Second, in the application of the metaphor the meanings of the terms of both the explanans and explanandum undergo change; this is a consequence of their interaction.

> The two systems are seen as more like each other; they seem to interact and adapt to one another, even to the point of invalidating their original literal descriptions if these are understood in the new, postmetaphoric sense.[29]
>
> Literal meanings are shifted by their association with metaphors. . . .[30]

According to the metaphorical view of explanation, then, there is a literal description of both the explanans and the explanandum. However language is used metaphorically when words ordinarily used in the literal description of the explanans are transferred to the explanandum. In this transfer the meanings of the terms of both the explanans and the explanandum undergo change; they come to be seen as analogous. Explanation essentially consists in a metaphorical redescription of the explanandum.

The metaphorical view of explanation has been put forward as an attempt to "modify" and "supplement" the deductive model. However there are important differences between the interaction view and the deductive model. First, the role of deduction becomes auxiliary on the metaphorical view. Second, the metaphorical view does away with the troublesome bifurcation of theoretical and observational language (and hence the need for the introduction of correspondence rules to connect the two). In the metaphorical view there is only one language—the observational.[31] Third, the metaphorical view provides for a strong sense of prediction—that is, prediction in which new observation predicates are added.[32] It is also clear that the metaphorical view of explanation constitutes a rejection of meaning invariance.

The introduction of the notion of metaphor is merely a necessary (not sufficient) modification of the deductive pattern of explanation. Not all metaphors explain. "Metaphor becomes explanatory only when its satisfies certain further conditions."[33] A necessary condition required

118

for explanation is that of analogy. Let us consider the introduction of analogy into metaphorical explanation and relate both to the role of theories.

We have already seen in the discussion of "valid inductive inference" (section 21) that Hesse rejects the view that theories are arranged in layers such that higher levels are generalizations from lower ones and allow predictions on the lower levels to be deduced. An example of a deductive structure such as she is rejecting is the following:[34]

Atomic and electronic theories of quantum mechanics
Theories of interaction between electromagnetic waves and material substances
Maxwell's principles of electrodynamics
Wave theory of light
Snell's law
Lens functioning as a magnifying glass

Each layer explains the layer just beneath it in the deductive structure. This model corresponds to inference pattern (1) (section 21), and the difficulties it involves have already been pointed out. Hesse's view of theories, as we have seen, is that they "abstract" or "extract" analogies. In the "valid inductive inference" pattern:

> We are no longer concerned with a dubious inductive inference from e_1 up to t and down to e_2, but with a direct analogical inference from e_1 to e_2. And t does not provide the upper level of a deductive structure, but rather extracts the essence from e_1 and e_2, that is to say it reveals in these laws the relevant analogies in virtue of which we pass from one to the other inductively.[35]

An example will serve to clarify Hesse's meaning of the abstraction of analogy. She gives the following technical description of an explanation.[36] Let t be Newton's theory of gravitation, e_1 be Kepler's laws, and e_2 be a prediction that a body in the neighborhood of the earth will

119

fall with a certain acceleration. Further let F, G, H represent properties of planets and P, Q, R represent certain motions of these planets. Schematically, e_1 amounts to $(x) [(F(x) \cdot G(x)) \supset (P(x) \cdot Q(x))]$ and e_2 amounts to $(x) [(G(x) \cdot H(x)) \supset (Q(x) \cdot R(x))]$. G is what is shared in both cases, e.g., "solid," "massive," "opaque." But not all of the properties are shared; there are, for example, differences in "size," "shape," and "chemical composition." Schematically t may be represented in the following way: $(x) [(F(x) \supset P(x)) \cdot (G(x) \supset Q(x)) \cdot (H(x) \supset R(x))]$. t logically entails the conjunction $e_1 \cdot e_2$, but $e_1 \cdot e_2$ do not entail t; hence t is more general. The role of t is threefold. (1) t picks out predicates in common between intial evidence and prediction (G and Q in e_1 and e_2), (2) t relates these predicates in terms of a conditional statement $(G(x) \supset Q(x))$ and (3) t asserts that different properties (F, P, H, R) are explained by two different laws, one applying only to the domain of initial evidence, e_1; the other only to the domain of prediction, e_2.

An explanation does not usually include an explanation of all the differences in the two domains, although it usually includes an explanation of some of the differences. Hence t can be more simply construed as $(x) (G(x) \supset Q(x))$. It allows the direct analogical inference from e_1 to e_2. Theories, in general, perform this function. "Theories consist just in the abstraction of analogical laws from a large number of empirical systems."[37] Deduction is not the essential inference in the relationship between a theory and the laws it explains. Theories do not entail laws; rather theories pick out analogies between laws and show analogies between systems.

The function of theories can be related to the doctrine of metaphorical explanation. e_2 and e_2 constitute the explanandum; the theory t explains (constitutes the explanans) e_1 and e_2 metaphorically. $(x) (G(x) \supset Q(x))$ is the essence of the explanation. But by picking out the analogy of e_1 and e_2 the meanings of G and Q in t interact with those in e_1 and e_2, and there is a meaning shift. e_1 and e_2 cannot entail t because of this meaning shift: The meanings of G and Q are expanded in t; yet the expansion includes their use in e_1 and e_2. Hence t does entail e_1 and e_2. G and Q in t represent the "synoptic vision" referred to by Whitehead.

It is clear that analogy and prediction are bound together in this view of theories. Indeed it might be argued that prediction constitutes another necessary condition for a metaphor to be explanatory.[38] There is a sense in which this condition is redundant, for we have seen it is a consequence of the metaphorical view that prediction in the strong sense is accounted for. The meaning shift which occurs in the interaction of explanans and explanandum allows for the suggestion of new hypotheses which could not have been associated with the terms of the explanandum in the premetaphorical sense.[39] All metaphors allow for prediction. It would seem as if a metaphor would be termed explanatory only if the predictions were confirmed.

Hesse suggests that the metaphorical view of explanation is a modification and a supplementation of the deductive view. The metaphorical view, however, clearly is not to be identified with any of the other explanation patterns described in sections 23 and 24. The metaphorical view does introduce a certain amount of imprecision into the logic of explanation. This is not to say that metaphors are illogical; rather it stems from the vastness of the domain from which metaphors may be drawn.

27. Environment, metaphor, and explanation

The passages already quoted from Whitehead's writings (section 25) suffice to show the closeness of the organic to the metaphorical view of explanation. In the organic view the essence of explanation is not deductive but a "synoptic vision" gained in finding generic categories from restricted facts or laws. The abstraction of such categories is based on analogy yet involves new meaning. The ordinary usage of terms is stretched in the generalization. The stretching suggests application of the category beyond the facts or laws from which it arose. A coherent set of generic categories constitutes a theory. The theory is essentially an abstraction of analogies between systems. Theories in science abstract analogies between more special systems; metaphysical theories abstract analogies between more general systems, e.g., the sciences themselves.

It is clear that the explanatory function of metaphor turns on the stretching of language by the metaphor. This stretching is made possible by analogy and makes possible new hypotheses. The necessary condition of analogy raises the question as to further (metaphysical) necessary conditions. We have already seen (section 22) that the inference potential of analogy is grounded in the notion of environment and the internal relations between an organism and the environment which sustains it. This suggests that the stretching of language is dependent upon the environment as well. Whitehead indeed maintained that meaning is environmentally dependent.

> Every science must devise its own instruments. The tool required for philosophy is language. Thus philosophy redesigns language in the same way that, in a physical science, pre-existing appliances are redesigned. It is exactly at this point that the appeal to facts is a difficult operation. This appeal is not solely to the expression of the facts in current verbal statements. The adequacy of such sentences is the main question at issue. It is true that the general agreement of mankind as to experienced facts is best expressed in language. But the language of literature breaks down precisely at the task of expressing in explicit form the larger generalities—the very generalities which metaphysics seeks to express.
>
> The point is that every proposition refers to a universe exhibiting some general systematic metaphysical character. Apart from this background, the separate entities which go to form the proposition, and the proposition as a whole, are without determinate character. Nothing has been defined, because every definite entity requires a systematic universe to supply its requisite status. Thus every proposition proposing a fact must, in its complete analysis, propose the general character of the universe required for that fact. There are no self-sustained facts, floating in nonentity. . . . A proposition can embody partial truth because it only demands a certain type of systematic environment, which is presupposed in its meaning. It does not refer to the universe in all its detail (PR 16-17).
>
> Language is thoroughly indeterminate, by reason of the fact that every occurrence presupposes some systematic type of environment (PR 18).

The dependence of meaning on a presupposed environment explains how the stretching of meaning in a metaphor is possible. It is possible because the extended meaning depends, not upon the original environment presupposed for the original meaning, but upon a different environment presupposed for the stretched meaning.

> Learned people have handled the specialization of thought with an incredible lack of precaution. It is almost universally assumed that the growth of a specialism leaves unaffected the presuppositions as to the perspective of the environment which were sufficient for the initial stages. It cannot be too clearly understood that the expansion of any special topic changes its whole meaning from top to bottom. As the subject matter of a science expands, its relevance to the universe contracts. For it presupposes a more strictly defined environment (MT 76-77).

122

The change in the presupposed environment brings with it changes in the presupposed dominant order. This shift in environmental order underlies the suggestiveness of the metaphor; the new dominant order makes possible new associations of meanings—associations not possible prior to the metaphor. Such associations were not possible because they were not included in the systematic associations of meanings in the original environment. They are not possible because of such systematic associations in the new environment.

Hence the role of metaphor in explanation depends not only upon analogy, but also upon the more detailed specification of the presupposed environment brought about in the stretching of meaning by the metaphorical use of language. The organic view of explanation, then, is in agreement with the metaphorical view of explanation and its proposed modifications of the deductive paradigm of explanation. The organic view provides, in addition, the metaphysical categories necessary to justify the metaphorical use of language in explanation.

X. Conceptual Change

28. Explanation and conceptual change

What is fundamentally at issue in the discussion of conceptual change is the relationship of an accepted theory in a given field to a theory which, in some sense, displaces it or becomes its successor. An understanding is being sought of the process of succession. A basic question is whether or not the relationship involves an explanation of the earlier theory by its successor. Hence a theory of explanation has direct relevance for a theory of conceptual change. In brief, those schools of thought which maintain that there is a logic of explanation can apply that logic to the pattern of explanation of the earlier theory by the later one. This pattern of explanation will elucidate the process of the change.

Then the formalists will have a deductive model of conceptual change, and the organicists will have a metaphorical model. It is with the historical relativist tradition that acute problems arise for understanding conceptual change. We have seen that their view of explanation (section 24) rejected a logic of explanation in favor of an analysis of particular situations of explanations to discern the procedures involved. In keeping with this procedural account, their view of conceptual change maintains that any particular example of conceptual change must be studied to see what factors brought about the change. These factors may be expected to vary from one situation to the next; in no sense can it be claimed that there is a transcendent set of reasons underlying the change in conceptual framework. This thesis allows for a range of views within the historical relativist tradition which will be noted in section 29. However before exploring the complexity of the historical relativist view, the formalist view of conceptual change needs to be set out, for it is this view which the historical relativists explicitly reject.

We have seen that the formalists make a radical distinction between

124

observational and theoretical language (section 23). Most formalists hold that there is no criterion for distinguishing what is "observable" from what is "not observable."[1] Yet they maintain that a criterion can be given for distinguishing descriptive terms which appear in experimental laws from descriptive terms which appear in theories.[2] It is this distinction which is being referred to in the dichotomy of language into the observational and the theoretical. The distinction is this: the descriptive terms of experimental laws, but not of theories, can be associated with (observable properties or) at least one experimental procedure. The procedure gives the term a fixed meaning, although its occurrence in any one particular law will likely determine only partial meaning. The descriptive term does not owe its meaning to its occurrence in the law. Its meaning can be thought of, rather, as the sum of all procedures that can be associated with it in every context in which it occurs. Hence the descriptive terms of experimental laws have meaning independent of the law, and the meaning of these terms does not change as they appear in different laws.[3] Then in the explanation of a law by a theory (1) the meaning of the terms of the law is independent of its incorporation into the theory. (2) If the theory is falsified or found unfruitful, the law can be maintained, because it continues to be supported by the original evidence which led to its formulation.[4] "Such facts indicate that an experimental law has, so to speak, a life of its own, not contingent on the continued life of any particular theory that may explain the law."[5]

Theoretical terms, on the other hand, derive meaning from two sources. First, they are implicitly defined by the theory in which they appear. The theory is conceived as analogous to an uninterpreted axiom system or calculus. This implicit definition is set by the relationship of the terms in the theory; it consists in delimiting the range of possible meanings which the term may take on. It is clear that a change in theory will bring about a change in the meanings of the theoretical terms if their relationships to one another are altered in the theoretical change.[6] Second, theoretical terms receive meaning from observational terms. This is because the uninterpreted calculus cannot have importance for science; its theoretical terms must be interpreted by correspondence rules which link the terms to experimental properties or procedures.[7] It is this latter source of meaning for theoretical terms which is being referred to when it is maintained that theoretical terms are given meaning by observational terms. Since the meanings of the observational terms are prior to and independent of the theory, successive (or competing) theories do not give different meaning to observational statements. This is the thesis of meaning invariance discussed in section 24.

The distinction between observational and theoretical language allows conceptual change to be explained by the deductive model. The meanings of the terms of the two theories are fixed. Hence an earlier theory can be explained by its successor by deducing it from the later theory and statements about the domain of application.[8] Conceptual change is, in essence, cumulative.

29. Paradigms, meaning variance, and scientific revolutions

The historical relativist position(s) on conceptual change will be discussed in the form in which it has been raised by T. S. Kuhn.[9] Kuhn has maintained that there are two aspects of scientific activity—normal and revolutionary—which differ in kind and not merely in degree. Normal science is governed by a paradigm, that is, by a set of shared commitments—symbolic generalizations, models, values, and concrete problem solutions.[10] These commitments prevent normal science from accounting for conceptual change. Conceptual change must be accounted for by revolutionary science. Revolutions occur when the shared commitments no longer provide an adequate methodology. In such times there is a lack of agreement as to commitments, and critical discussion ensues. A revolution ends with the choice of a new paradigm. The methodology prescribed by the new paradigm begins a new period of normal science.

Among the functions of a paradigm is the determination of relevant observations.[11] We have seen (section 20) that Kuhn and others have interpreted this determination to entail a thesis about the meaning of scientific terms, *viz.,* the meaning of scientific terms depends upon a theoretical framework. This thesis constitutes a reversal of the formalist view of the roles of observational and theoretical language and has been referred to in the previous chapter as that of "meaning variance." This thesis admits of a plurality of interpretations. The disagreement that is important to our discussion is with respect to whether or not some terms are invariant when a paradigm change, or revolution, occurs. The revolutionary theory of conceptual change advanced by Kuhn seems to maintain that no terms are invariant with respect to such change—a change of theoretical framework entails a change of meaning for every term in the theory. This revolutionary theory of conceptual change has come under widespread attack, even by those who wish to maintain some interpretation of the meaning variance thesis. These philosophers have pointed out difficulties for the revolutionary theory of conceptual change and have circumvented the difficulties by claiming the independence of the theses of meaning variance and revolutionary conceptual change. In the remainder of this section some of these difficulties will be enumerated. The following section will be concerned with sketching Whitehead's position with respect to the basic theses at issue.

(1) One difficulty is how to distinguish the kind of extension and articulation of a theory which is the concern of normal science from revolutionary conceptual change. Critics have demanded a criterion for change of meaning in asking the following questions: cannot any conceptual change (including theory extension-articulation) count as a micro-revolution?[12] Is it possible to say that the meaning is the same, but the application of the term has changed?[13]

(2) Another difficulty is how to conceive of the relationship of the "same" term in successive theories.[14] Does the revolutionary theory of conceptual change entail that the term in T* is discontinuous with the "same" term in its successor T? If so, how could one ever come to understand T, since the meanings of the "same" terms in T are unrelated to the meanings in T*.[15]

(3) A third difficulty is that the revolutionary theory of conceptual change seems to entail the impossibility of successive theories being conceived as rival theories because some commonness of meaning is presupposed for the theories to have incompatible hypotheses.[16]

An attempt will be made to answer these difficulties in considering Kuhn's clarification of the notion of scientific revolutions in sections 31 and 32.

30. The organic categories for the structure of scientific revolutions

Although one does not find the terms "normal science," "revolutionary science," "paradigm," "theory-laden observation," "meaning variance," etc., in Whitehead's writings, there are clear refereneces to analogues of the doctrines for which they stand.

(1) The distinction between normal and revolutionary science:[17]

> The advance of any reasonably developed science is two-fold. There is the advance of detailed knowledge within the method prescribed by the reigning working hypothesis; and there is the rectification of the working hypothesis dictated by the inadequacies of the current orthodoxy (AI 286).

(2) Normal science is characterized by the absence of critical discussion.[18]

> A philosophic system . . . is rarely of any direct importance for particular sciences. Each such science in tracing its ideas backward to their basic notions stops at a half-way house. It finds a resting place amid notions which for its immediate purposes and its immediate methods it need not analyze any further (AI 184).

> The field of a special science is confined to one genus of facts, in the sense that no statements are made respecting facts which lie outside that genus. . . .

> The study of philosophy is a voyage toward the larger generalities. For this reason in the infancy of science, when the main stress lay in the discovery of the most general ideas usefully applicable to the subject-matter in question, philosophy was not sharply distinguished from science. To this day, a new science with any substantial novelty in its notions is considered to be in some way peculiarly philosophical. In their later stages, apart from occasional disturbances most sciences accept without question the general notions in terms of which they develop. The main stress is laid on the adjustment and the direct verification of more special statements. In such periods scientists repudiate philosophy. . . (PR 14-15).

(3) Normal scientific activity is determined by a paradigm whose function it is to prescribe method:[19]

> No systematic thought has made progress apart from some adequately general working hypothesis, adapted to its special topic. Such an hypothesis directs observation, and decides upon the mutual relevance of various types of evidence. In short, it prescribes method (AI 286).

(4) Meaning variance is accepted; the meaning of scientific terms depends upon a theoretical framework:[20]

> So far as concerns methodology, the general issue of the discussion will be that theory dictates method, and that any particular method is only applicable to theories of one correlate species. An analogous conclusion holds for the technical terms. This close relation of theory to method partly arises from the fact that relevance of evidence depends on the theory which is dominating the discussion. This fact is the reason why dominant theories are also termed 'working hypotheses' (AI 283).

> Our coordinated knowledge, which in the general sense of the term is Science, is formed by the meeting of two orders of experience. One order is constituted by the direct, immediate discriminations of particular observations (Observational Order). The other order is constituted by our general way of conceiving the universe (Conceptual Order). . . . The observational order is invariably interpreted in terms of the concepts supplied by the conceptual order (AI 198).

(5) Observation is theory-laden in the strong sense; it is not merely that under two paradigms the same facts are seen but interpreted differently:[21]

> The question as to the priority of one or the other [observational order, conceptual order] is, for the purposes of this discussion, academic. We inherit an observational order, namely types of things which we do in fact discriminate; and we inherit a conceptual order, namely a rough system of ideas in terms of which we do in fact interpret. We can point to no epoch in human history, or even in animal history, at which this interplay began. Also it is true that novel observations modify the conceptual order. But equally, novel concepts suggest novel possibilities of observational discrimination (AI 198).

(6) Because of the theory-ladenness of observations, verification and falsification apply only to testing within normal science and not between successive paradigms:[22]

> You cannot prove a theory by evidence which that theory dismisses as irrelevant. This is also the reason that in any science which has failed to produce any theory with a sufficient scope of application, progress is necessarily very slow. It is impossible to know what to look for, and how to correct the sporadic observations (AI 284).

> When a new working hypothesis is proposed, it must be criticized from its own point of view. For example, it is futile to object to the Newtonian dynamics that, on the Aristotelian system the loose things on the earth's surface must be left behind by the earth's motion (AI 286).

These passages suffice to show the closeness of Whitehead's categories of conceptual change to those of Kuhn. The questions that must now be considered are whether or not these categories entail a revolutionary theory of conceptual change, and, if so, how such a theory can handle the difficulties raised in section 24.

31. Revolutionary conceptual change

Kuhn has claimed that the theses of meaning variance and revolutionary conceptual change are dependent. Other philosophers have maintained that even though the meaning of scientific terms depends on a framework, a change in framework may involve a change of meaning for every term in the theory, but also may involve a change for some, but not for others.[23] This latter claim is not a contradiction in terms. Hence it seems that the thesis of revolutionary conceptual change follows from meaning variance only if another premise is added. The suppressed premise seems to be that the change in theoretical framework is absolute —there is *no relationship* of the terms in the new framework to those of the original framework. This premise, however, makes it impossible to answer the second of the difficulties raised in section 29. There can be no continuity of the "same" terms in successive theories and the change is completely unintelligible.[24] Yet Kuhn is not willing to maintain this radical thesis.[25] Meaning change is not of the nature of deduction, but it is intelligible all the same. What seems to be needed is a clarification of the phrase "change in theoretical framework" in the statement that a change in theoretical framework involves a change of meaning for every term of the theory. I think it can be argued that Kuhn does not hold this change in theoretical framework to be absolute.

In his detailed discussion of the conceptual transformation involved in the change from Newtonian to Einsteinian paradigms in physics,[26] he emphasizes the "subtleness" of the revolution (on the whole the same terminology was retained and the universe was populated by the same entities), yet cites it as a "prototype for revolutionary orientation in the sciences."[27] Although he is clear that the acceptance of the Einsteinian paradigm constituted a "decisive destruction" of the Newtonian, he

130

describes this "decisive destruction" by a particularly enlightening term, *viz.,* "displacement": this revolution "illustrates with particular clarity the scientific revolution as a displacement of the conceptual network through which scientists view the world."[28]

The term "displacement" suggests that there is not an absolute change in successive paradigms. "Displacement" presupposes a connection with that which is displaced, and, thus, the possibility of a description of this connection. An absolute change, a discontinuous change, on the other hand, would be a "replacement" of one paradigm by another. Such a "replacement" would constitute an unintelligible change, and this is not Kuhn's meaning.

How is one to understand this "displacment"? The key passage for the elucidation of this term is, I think, the following:

> One of the things upon which the practice of normal science depends is a learned ability to group objects and situations into similarity classes which are primitive in the sense that the grouping is done without an answer to the question, 'similar with respect to what?' One aspect of every revolution is, then, that some of the similarity relations change. Objects which were grouped in the same set before are grouped in different sets afterwards and *vice-versa.* . . . Since most objects within even the altered sets continue to be grouped together, the names of the sets are generally preserved. Nevertheless, the transfer of a subset can crucially affect the network of interrelations among sets.[29]

This passage is reiterated, with only minimal change in the wording, in the "Postscript" to *The Structure of Scientific Revolutions.*[30] I suggest that Kuhn is maintaining that the displacement primarily refers to a change in the analogy and similarity relationships in the conceptual network.

The implication of this notion of displacement for the meaning of the "same" term in successive theories is that there is not a discontinuity nor an absolute change in meaning. There is rather a meaning shift, whose degree varies with the shift in relations the term has to other terms in the theory after displacement.

> In the transition from one theory to the next words change their meanings or conditions of applicability in subtle ways. Though most of the same signs are used before and after a revolution—e.g. force, mass, element, compound, cell—the ways in which some of them attach to nature has somehow changed.[31]

The change in the ways terms attach to nature is a function of change in positive and negative analogies seen in nature brought about by the conceptual change. New conceptual knots tie together phenomena not previously related because their positive analogy was not recognized; other conceptual knots are unloosed because the new network suggests the phenomena involved have more negative than positive analogy.

This account gives some clarification to the "change in theoretical framework" which constitutes a revolutionary conceptual change. The kind of change that is meant is a displacement in the conceptual framework, and the displacement can be characterized as a change in analogies and similarity relationships. In the displacement of a conceptual framework, the meanings of terms can be extended or stretched. An account of this displacement and stretching has been given by philosophers advocating the metaphorical view of scientific explanation. We have seen that the organic philosophy is in agreement with this view of explanation. The organic view of conceptual change can also be developed in conjunction with theirs.

32. Metaphor and conceptual change

We have seen (sections 26 and 27) how explanatory categories in science can be conceived as metaphors. This view of scientific explanation has built into it a mechanism for conceptual change by way of metaphor.[32] The same features which account for the explanatory function of metaphor account for the possibility of intelligible conceptual change. These features are (a) the positive analogy of the term in T* and its successor T and (b) the hypothesis-producing potential of placing the term from T* into the displaced framework T. Without (a) there seems to be no possibility of understanding the meaning of terms which appear in both theories. The analogies between the terms in T* and T make possible the understanding of the real meaning of the term in T. Without (b) no sense can be made of a real change in meaning. The hypotheses suggested by this aspect of the metaphor lead to the development of the framework which gives the term its new meaning.

> When we first consider a term like "length" in the mechanics of relativity, its meaning is derived from classical mechanics and it seems absurd to us to take a

fixed measurable entity and view it "as if" it were relative to velocity. The new meaning of "length" is suggested by its theoretical context and we are asked to consider it as an hypothesis. An old familiar term is used in a new way; it is a metaphor and that enables us to recognize it as intelligible and yet still consider a possible new connotation for it is its hypothetical or "as if" quality. Soon evidence is presented to corroborate the new hypothetical meaning and falsify the old notion. As the meaning of "length" in relativity becomes commonplace, it ceases to be a metaphor.[33]

The meaning is changed because the term has a different association with the other terms in the respective frameworks. In T* no association is made between length and velocity. In T such an association is made. This association suggests other possibilities for association in the displaced framework.

This view of conceptual change does not involve the difficulties enumerated in section 29.

(1') A criterion for a change in meaning can be given: it is a necessary condition for a change in meaning that the analogies of the theoretical framework change. This allows for the distinction between the extension/articulation of the theoretical framework which goes on in normal science and the real meaning change in the framework displacement in revolutionary science. The former does not involve a change in the associations of the terms, while the latter does. A change in the application of a term seems to be at the same time a change in meaning, as Kuhn suggests.[34] Such a change presupposes the new associations which are the mark of conceptual change.

(2') Sense can be made of the relationship of the "same" term in successive theories: T*, T. The meanings of the "same" terms are given continuity by the positive analogy of the terms in both theoretical frameworks. It is just because of this analogy that it makes sense to use the same sign in both frameworks. The meaning of the term T*, which depends on its relationships with the other terms in T*, is the basis for the extended meaning of the term in T.

(3') T* and T can be considered rival theories because there is a commonness of meaning of the "same" terms in both.

The metaphorical view of conceptual change is completely in accord with Whitehead's view of explanation and meaning. Hence in spite of the acceptance of "paradigm," "normal-revolutionary science," "theory-ladenness of observation," "meaning variance," Whitehead is not committed to the doctrine of revolutionary conceptual change. For the organic philosophy change is never absolute; there is continuity between successive theoretical frameworks. In the terminology of the first four chapters of this work:

(1'') The criterion for a change in meaning is the necessary changed environment presupposed for the existence of the novel facts.

(2'') There is a continuity between successive environments. E is analogically inferred from E* on the basis of the analogies between the facts of each.

(3'') Environmental orders can be incompatible. Whitehead's insistence that

> Words and phrases must be stretched toward a generality foreign to their ordinary usage; and however such elements of language be stabilized as technicalities, they remain metaphors mutely appealing for an imaginative leap (PR 6).

is an insistence that successive frameworks are not incommensurable. The meanings of a term in T* and T are not incommensurable because stretching is essentially the grasping of a clearer generic meaning of which the meanings in T* are species. Successor theories represent "synoptic vision" with respect to meaning. But because a more adequate generic meaning of the term is reached in T, it is possible to hold T* and T as "not both true"—i.e., incompatible. When wider meanings are found, there is no reason to think the narrower meanings adequate (true). The theoretical framework constituting these meanings is in this sense incompatible with the framework determining the wider meanings.

33. Theory choice: realism vs. instrumentalism

The thesis of meaning variance has also been taken to entail a kind of irrationality in the choice of a new theoretical framework, because a rational choice would seem to depend upon some commonness of meaning.

We have seen that Kuhn's clarification of theoretical change is compatible with views which find such a commonness of meaning by conceiving of scientific terms as metaphors. This weakens, but does not eliminate, the factor of irrationality in theory choice. Kuhn gives a clarification of the meaning of this irrationality: "In a debate over choice of theory, neither party has access to an argument which resembles a proof in logic or formal mathematics."[35] Such a proof would presuppose agreement as to the premises, rules of inference and proof procedure. The proof procedure guarantees that if there is disagreement about the conclusion, a check can be made after which one party to the disagreement changes his mind. Theory choice in science is not like this. The proof procedure, premises, and rules of inference are themselves paradigm-bound.[36] However this thesis is not an especially strong one; it is too weak to entail that scientists do not use logic in theory choice. It only entails that their arguments for theory choice are not compelling.[37] It is strong enough to suggest that in the absence of such compelling logical arguments, persuasion may be involved in choice. But Kuhn insists that persuasion can include good reasons: accuracy, scope, simplicity, fruitfulness.[38] Kuhn prefers to call these "values" in the determination of an acceptable theory. They represent a kind of invariance in conceptual change, but not a strict invariance—their application can be construed differently by parties to a dispute about theory choice; and, when applied together, they may be liable to conflict. Finally, the kind of irrationalism Kuhn is maintaining is too weak to entail relativism—that any theory is as good as any other.[39] But Kuhn does hedge with respect to the thesis that scientific theories represent an approach to the truth.

> Nevertheless, there is another step, or kind of step, which many philosophers of science wish to take and which I refuse. They wish, that is, to compare theories as representations of nature, as statements about 'what is really out there'. Granting that neither theory of a historical pair is true, they nonetheless seek a sense in which the latter is a better approximation to the truth. I believe nothing of that sort can be found.[40]

Kuhn takes this stand principally because he believes that the succession of theories does not reveal direction in ontological development.

> To say, for example, of a field theory that it 'approaches more closely to the truth' than an older matter-and-force theory should mean, unless words are being oddly used, that the ultimate constituents of nature are more like fields

135

than like matter and force. But in this ontological context it is far from clear how the phrase 'more like' is to be applied. Comparison of historical theories gives no sense that their ontologies are approaching a limit; in some fundamental ways Einstein's general relativity resembles Aristotle's physics more than Newton's.[41]

This is a reiteration of the conclusion of *The Structure of Scientific Revolutions* that progress is progress-from-what-we-do-know not progress-toward-what-we-want-to-know.[42]

Here Kuhn is rejecting a realist interpretation of scientific theories in favor of an instrumentalist one. These views have been traditionally distinguished in the following ways: (1) realism maintains that statements of a scientific theory are true or false; instrumentalism maintains that truth value is not applicable to theoretical statements, rather these statements are to be construed as instruments for the ordering of observations and of experimental laws. (2) Realism maintains that theoretical statements function as the premises of a deduction; instrumentalism maintains that theoretical statements play the role of the inference rules of a deduction.[43] Another mode of distinguishing the two views has been necessitated by the debate between formalists and historical relativists over the thesis of meaning variance. (3) For realists, but not for instrumentalists, scientific knowledge must, in some sense, have a cumulative character.[44]

It is sufficiently clear that the organic philosophy requires a realist interpretation of scientific theories. Three main reasons can be offered for this conclusion. First, Whitehead maintained a thoroughgoing scientific realism in both his early and late writings in his arguments against the positivist interpretation of theoretical statements as mere descriptions (CN 45-46; FR 54-58). Indeed he took the denial of realism to be an instance of the "bifurcation of nature."

> The most attenuated form which the bifurcation theory assumes, is to maintain that the molecules and ether of science are purely conceptual. Thus there is but one nature, namely apparent nature, and atoms and ether are merely names for logical terms in conceptual formulae of calculation.
>
> But what is a formula of calculation? It is presumably a statement that something or other is true for natural occurrences. . . . Now if there are no such entities, I fail to see how any statement about them can apply to nature. For example, the assertion that there is green cheese in the moon cannot be a premise in any deduction of scientific importance, unless indeed the presence of

green cheese in the moon has been verified by experiment. The current answer to these objections is that, though atoms are merely conceptual, yet they are an interesting and picturesque way of saying something else which is true of nature. But surely if it is something else that you mean, for heaven's sake say it. Do away with this elaborate machinery of a conceptual nature which consists of assertions about things which don't exist in order to convey truths about things which do exist. I am maintaining the obvious position that scientific laws, if they are true, are statements about entities which we obtain knowledge of as being in nature; and that, if the entities to which the statements refer are not to be found in nature, the statements about them have no relevance to any purely natural occurrence. Thus the molecules and electrons of scientific theory are, so far as science has correctly formulated its laws, each of them factors to be found in nature. The electrons are only hypothetical in so far as we are not quite certain that the electron theory is true. But their hypothetical character does not arise from the essential nature of the theory in itself after its truth has been granted (CN 45-46).

Second, we have seen that the organic view of laws entails a scientific realism. "By the doctrine of Law as immanent it is meant that the order of nature expresses the characters of the real things which jointly compose the existences to be found in nature" (AI 142). Third, the explication of "valid inductive inference," in which theories make possible the inductive inferences between data and prediction, presupposes a realist interpretation of scientific theories. This is because a theory must be interpreted as an observable model to pick out the analogies, and hence its statements must have truth value.[45] The organic philosophy strengthens the presupposition of realism in "valid inductive inference" by maintaining that the pattern is not valid unless the internal relatedness between the organisms and environments constituting the physical world be admitted.

It has been argued that the two traditional ways of distinguishing realism and instrumentalism can be interpreted so as to reduce the distinction to one of degree and not of kind.[46] It is, therefore, the third, and relatively recent, distinction which requires discussion. Indeed the possibility of the cumulative character of scientific theories is precisely what Kuhn is getting at in his demand to make sense of direction of ontological development. The issue of meaning variance entails that "cumulation" cannot be meant in the simple sense of the formalists.

The organic philosophy does accept a version of the thesis of meaning variance. Hence it must show how a realist position may be maintained

137

in cases where competing or successor theories containing quite different concepts are being compared. Hesse considers the following three cases to be the most difficult for realists to handle.[47] If T*, T represent competing theories:

(1) T*, T presuppose different "ontologies of individuals," yet both are probable theories.

(2) T*, T presuppose the same "ontology of individuals," but at least some statements of the two theories seem to contradict one another.

If T*, T represent successive theories:

(3) T*, T presuppose different "ontologies of individuals;" T* is displaced by T.

In considering these cases it needs to be remarked that the "individuals" whose ontological status is being referred to are the complex organisms Whitehead calls societies. The characteristics sustained by societies can and do change.

Case (1) is exemplified by the particle/wave duality in the theory of light. Whitehead explicitly discussed this duality in terms of the characteristics of social order. He explained the duality by the theses of the incompleteness of order in any society and by the change in dominant order that is continuously, though perhaps slowly, going on in most (or all) societies.

> For example, the doctrine, here explained, conciliates Newton's corpuscular theory of light with the wave theory. For both a corpuscle, and an advancing element of wave front, are merely a permanent form propagated from atomic creature [primary organism] to atomic creature [primary organism]. A corpuscle is in fact an 'enduring object.' The notion of an 'enduring object' is, however, capable of more or less completeness of realization. Thus, in different stages of its career, a wave of light may be more or less corpuscular. A train of such waves at all stages of its career involves social order; but in the earlier stages this social order takes the more special form of loosely related strands of personal order. This dominant personal order gradually vanishes as the time advances. Its defining characteristics become less and less important, as their various features peter out. The waves then become a nexus with important social order, but with no strands of personal order. Thus the train of waves starts up as a corpuscular society, and ends as a society which is not corpuscular (PR 53-54).

Case (2) is explained by the doctrine of the incompleteness of social order. There is order, but there is also disorder. If T* and T represent

138

different theories, and their role is the abstraction of analogies between laws, the analogies abstracted by each will not be exactly the same. Then it is to be expected that some of the less general statements implied by T* will differ significantly from those implied by T. Indeed the less general statements may seem to contradict one another. In other terms, a very general environment containing more special environments may have many theories explaining the laws of the more special environments which relate different sets of statistical laws in these more special environments. Since a general environment can tolerate a wide range of disorder, incompatible statements may be derived from these theories.

Case (3) is at the heart of Kuhn's rejection of realism. What is being demanded by critics of realism is a "criterion of cumulation" which is consistent with both the thesis of realism and the thesis of meaning variance. Some account of ontological progress must be given.

Whitehead's clearest discussion of "progress through revolutions" in science is to be found in FR. There he maintains that the two aspects of reason, practical (scientific method) and speculative (metaphysical systems) are interrelated in such a way that progress results: scientific discoveries provide data for speculation; speculation produces an accumulation of theoretical frameworks which make possible the transition to new scientific methodologies when they are needed.

> The speculative Reason produces that accumulation of theoretical understanding which at critical moments enables a transition to be made toward new methodologies. Also the discoveries of practical understanding provide the raw material necessary for the success of the speculative Reason (FR 39).

The same point is made in AI:

> The collapse of nineteenth century dogmatism is a warning that the special sciences require that the imaginations of men be stored with imaginative possibilities as yet unutilized in the service of scientific explanation. The nearest analogy is to be seen in the history of some species of animal, or plant, or microbe, which lurks for ages as an obscure by-product of nature in some lonely jungle, or morass, or island. Then by some trick of circumstance it escapes into the outer world and transforms a civilization, or destroys an empire or the forests of a continent. Such is the potential power of the ideas which live in the various systems of philosophy (AI 186-87).

This understanding of the relationship between science and philosophy provides a much-needed answer to the question posed by Kuhn's critics as to the origin of new paradigms, given that critical thought is not the business of normal science.[48]

In addition to "proliferating possible paradigms," philosophy performs other tasks with respect to the special sciences. The most important of these is to be their critic and interpreter.

> It is the task of philosophy to work at the concordance of ideas conceived as illustrated in the concrete facts of the real world. It seeks those generalities which characterize the complete reality of fact, and apart from which any fact must sink into an abstraction. But science makes the abstraction, and is content to understand the complete fact in respect to only some of its essential aspects. Science and philosophy mutually criticize each other, and provide imaginative material for each other. A philosophic system should present an elucidation of concrete fact from which the sciences abstract. Also the sciences should find their principles in the concrete fact which a philosophic system presents (AI 187).

> In the absence of some understanding of the final nature of things, and thus of the sorts of backgrounds presupposed in such abstract statements, all science suffers from the vice that it may be combining various propositions which tacitly presuppose inconsistent backgrounds. No science can be more secure than the unconscious metaphysics which tacitly it presupposes. The individual thing is necessarily a modification of its environment, and cannot be understood in disjunction (AI 197).

I think these passages suggest an answer to Kuhn's requirement of evidence of ontological progress through scientific revolutions. Science and philosophy are aspects of the same human enterprise—to interpret experience in terms of a general conceptual system. Philosophy and science differ in that the conceptual systems provided by philosophy are more general and can, thus, criticize and interpret the systems of the sciences. But the systems of both science and philosophy develop in interaction. Successive theories in both science and philosophy involve a widening of explanatory categories—an extension of the meanings of terms—to catch ever more experience. There is ontological development in the sense that certain groups of experience can be seen as species of one general category. This constitutes the meaning of the "cumulative" aspect of scientific theories. The fact that there are presently categories which allow us to say that certain aspects of Aristotle's physics are closer to Einstein's than either is to Newton's shows the scientific categories have been widened to the point that the relationship of terms in the three theories can be understood.

140

There is, then, not only progress-from-what-we-do-know but also progress-towards-what-we-want-to-know. What-we-want-to-know are the categories which will systematize all experience. The history of science and philosophy does show a widening of these categories; this progression constitutes ontological development and makes the belief in scientific realism a justifiable one.

XI. Reduction

34. Theoretical reduction

The term "reduction" covers a complex set of interrelated issues which have received extensive discussion by the formalists. These issues center around two senses of reduction: (1) the reducibility of one science to another, or of one theory to another theory in the same field of a science,[1] and (2) the predictability in hierarchically structured wholes of properties at higher levels of organization from properties of lower levels of organization.[2] This section will briefly state the formalist conclusions with respect to each.

(1) It is widely agreed that the reduction of one science S* to another science S requires two formal conditions. First, since reduction in essence constitutes an explanation of the reduced by the reducing science, a condition of "derivability" is entailed by the formalist view of explanation: the theories and experimental laws of S* must be logically derivable from the theory of S.[3] Second, although the reduced science S* and the reducing science S have a larger number of expressions whose descriptive terms are associated with the same meanings, there are descriptive terms in S* which are not found in S. This situation entails the necessity of a "connectability condition." This condition requires that suitable linking or connecting principles be found to link the terms of S* with the terms of S. When these connecting principles are added to S as additional premises, the deduction of the laws of S* is then possible.[4] Clearly the "connectability condition" is the central problem of the formalist view of reduction. Formalists are in agreement that in most cases such connecting principles have not been found; their view is that it is in principle possible to find such connecting principles. The nature of the connecting principles has received much consideration. The alternatives for conceiving them are generally thought to be reducible to three: they constitute "logical connections" between the

meanings of terms in S* and S, they are "conventions,"[5] and/or they are "factual" or "material," i.e., there are situations describable by the terms of S which are necessary, sufficient, or necessary and sufficient for the application of the terms of S*.[6]

(2) In discussing the properties of different levels of a hierarchy, the predictablity (or unpredictability) referred to is the possibility of deducing one set of statements from another. The statements which constitute the premises of the deduction are those describing the "parts" of a "whole." The question is whether or not the properties of the parts (which differ from the properties of the whole they organize) in the specific relationship which organizes the whole suffice for the prediction of the properties of that whole.[7]

Formalists have argued that in many cases it is possible to predict properties of the whole from properties of parts. Examples of such prediction abound with respect to chemical compounds. In principle the properties of the compound can be deduced from the spectroscopic properties of the constituent atoms. In practice, however, this is not the usual procedure because of the complexity of the valency theory. But in principle the properties of the compound could be discovered without observation of the compound.[8]

However formalists also maintain that there is unpredictability in at least two important senses. First, the deduction in question is not possible when the premises are constituted merely of statements about the properties of the parts in that relationship. What must be added are premises elaborating a theory which describes the behavior of those parts in forming wholes. That is, from a statement of a theory describing generally the potentiality of parts to organize wholes and the statement of the condition of a particular organizing relation, a statement describing a whole with particular properties can be deduced. Second, the conclusion as to the properties of the whole may follow from one theory about the potential behavior of parts and the organizing relation in question and yet may not follow from another theory (and the same organizing relation).[9]

35. Paradigms and reduction

The historical relativist attack on the formalist view of reduction is centered on the first sense of reduction *viz.,* that of the reduction of one theory to another in the same field, or of one field of science to another field. Their argument against the formalist view of reduction is basically the same as the argument against a formal account of explanation.[10] It is maintained that the conditions which make a reduction possible cannot *in principle* be met. The condition of the connectability of terms occurring only in the reduced science S* with terms in S is not in general possible because of meaning variance. The meanings of the terms in S* depend upon the theories of S* and those of S depend upon the theories of S. The terms of S* cannot, then, be incorporated into S with unchanged meanings. The impossibility of satisfying the "connectability criterion" rules out the possibility of satisfying the "derivability criterion" as well. Without the connection of terms in S* and S, there can be no logically valid deduction of the laws of S* from those of S, and, hence, no formal reduction of S* to S.

Although historical relativists agree that a formal account of the reduction of one theory to another or of one science to another cannot be given, some have maintained that there is a sense in which one science or field of science can be a paradigm to another,[11] or that there is a sense in which one paradigm can be shared by a plurality of scientific fields.[12] Toulmin defends the former sense. We have seen that he maintains that there is a paradigm for any particular field of science which determines the explanatory procedures and the scope of these procedures (section 24). He claims, in addition, that one field of science S may be a paradigm to another field S* in the sense that S determines the explanatory procedures of S*. There is no formal reduction of S* to S, but a "subordination." "But, when we compare happenings of *different* kinds, we find different sciences being subordinated to one another, and so setting standards for one another. . . . Phenomena may, as a result, be explained . . . by relating them to happenings of some other sort, which are thought to be intrinsically more natural, acceptable, and self-explanatory."[13] Toulmin suggests that in explaining physical change prior to 1600, physiology was in some sense dominant to physics and chemistry; physical change was explained in terms of the mode of

144

development of the changing thing. The roles of dominance and sub-ordination were clearly reversed, however, after 1800. Then physiology became subordinate to physics and chemistry; the development of physical things tended to be explained, in so far as possible, in terms of the material components and their structure.[14] The subordination of one science to another is never a question of deducibility; indeed the roles of the two sciences may, in time, be reversed.

The sense in which a paradigm may be dominant for a plurality of fields is discussed by Kuhn. In defining a paradigm, Kuhn turns the emphasis away from fields with set subject-matters to groups or scientific communities with shared commitments. "A paradigm governs . . . not a subject matter but rather a group of practitioners."[15] "Some scientific subjects . . . have belonged to different scientific communities at different times, sometimes to several at once without becoming the province of any."[16] The paradigm, then, may be shared with other groups whose members pursue the solutions of puzzles which would seemingly be categorized as the subject-matter of different fields. The shared commitment may include any of the components of a paradigm: symbolic generalizations, models, values, exemplars. Exemplars offer some of the best historical examples of paradigms extending over a plurality of fields. Exemplars involve "learning from problems to see situations as like each other, as subjects for the application of the same scientific law or law-sketch."[17] Kuhn cites as an example Galileo's work on inclined planes, Huygen's work on the center of oscillation of a physical pendulum, and Bernoulli's work on the flow of water from an orifice as an application of one symbolic generalization *(vis viva)* to different subject-matters.[18] In this sense, then one paradigm may be shared by groups of practitioners in different fields. It is clear that neither the subordination of some paradigms to others nor the extension of paradigms over more than one field constitute reductions of one paradigm to another.

36. The unity of nature: mechanism vs. organicism

The acceptance of a logic of explanation suggests that some sense of a reduction of one theory (or science) to another is possible. However since the organic pattern of explanation is not a deductive one, the formalist requirement of derivability is not met simply by virtue of the existence of a logic of explanation. In the organic view explanation is metaphorical explanation; hence at first glance a theory (science) may be metaphorically reducible to another, but not deductively reducible.

On the other hand it seems that a stronger sense of reduction might be defended by the organic view. This is suggested by the doctrine that all sciences study organisms. "Biology is the study of larger organisms; whereas physics is the study of the smaller organisms" (SMW 150). What is being maintained here is a certain unity in the subject-matter of all natural science and the possibility of reducing the laws of one science to those of another because of the commonness of this subject-matter. This commonness eliminates, in many cases, the need for connecting principles between the terms of two sciences. This doctrine also entails the impossibility, in the organic view, of separating senses (1) and (2) of reduction. The formal reducibility of one theory (or science) to another depends upon the deducibility of properties of higher organisms from lower organisms which constitute them. The question of reduction, then, ultimately turns on the whole-part relationship of organisms. In this section the sense in which this relationship can be understood in terms of deducibility will be considered.

Formalists maintain that, in principle, biology is reducible to physics and chemistry; that is, the laws governing living organisms are derivable from those governing their physico-chemical parts (when the suitable connections are made between terms which appear to be exclusively biological and certain physico-chemical structures or events).[19] In addition they take this sense of the reduction of biology to physics and chemistry to entail a number of theses about the whole-part relationship in organisms. Of these theses I take the following four to be the most important.

M-1   Organisms are not more than the sum of their physico-chemical parts.

M-2   The understanding of an organism can be achieved (in principle) by a full understanding of the physico-chemical parts of the organism.

M-3   The physico-chemical parts determine the nature of the organism.

M-4   Organisms can be adequately studied by analytical methods.

These theses constitute the basis of a mechanistic understanding of organisms.

The organic philosophy maintains the internal relatedness of organisms and their environment and, since an organism may be considered an environment to its constituent organisms, the whole-part relationship of organisms must be conceived in terms of internal relatedness. Formalists have maintained that this internal relatedness commits the organicist to theses which are contraries to the mechanistic ones, *viz.,*

O-1   Organisms are more than the sums of their physico-chemical parts.

O-2   The understanding of an organism cannot be achieved by a full understanding of its physico-chemical parts in isolation from the organism.

O-3   The organism determines the nature of its physico-chemical parts.

O-4   The complexity and hierarchical organization of organisms precludes an adequate understanding by analytical methods.

I wish to examine these claims in succession. Each set is related in such a way that all four claims must be accepted if any one is. This makes a truly independent examination of the claims an impossibility.

M-1 vs. O-1:

Organicists base the claim of the irreducibility of organisms to sums of physico-chemical parts on the evidence that such parts, say, i, j, and k, may behave differently in isolation than they behave when they organize a complex C.[20] The organicist has sometimes been interpreted as meaning that i exhibits "new characters" in C—characters not found to be predicable of i in isolation. "New characters" is a somewhat ambiguous notion. If it is taken to mean characters for which there is no ground in the isolated part i,[21] the organicist is put in the position of being logically absurd, resorting to "miracles."[22] But there is another way of construing "new characters," *viz.,* that these characters are potentially predicable

147

of i in isolation which become actually predicable of i when i, j, and k organize complex C. This meaning of "new characters" is not logically absurd, and it is in complete accord with the empirical evidence on which the organicist claim is based.

Contemporary mechanists do not mean organisms are mere aggregates when they claim the reducibility of organisms to "sums" of physico-chemical parts. Nagel's discussion of the meaning of "sum" is most illuminating.[23] Consider i, j, and k organizing complex C. C is a sum of i, j, and k, if the theories which explain isolated i, isolated j, and isolated k (T-i, T-j, T-k) explains the behavior of i, j, and k in complex C. More precisely, C is the sum of i, j, and k, if one can deduce from T-i, T-j, and T-k the laws explaining the properties of i, j, and k in C. On the other hand C is not a sum of i, j, and k, if one cannot deduce these laws from T-i, T-j, and T-k. In such cases a wider theory T* is needed to explain the behavior of i, j, and k in C. Nagel concludes that whether or not any complex is a sum of its parts is *relative to a theory*. In brief, a complex is a sum when theories about its parts explain the relationship of the parts in the complex but not a sum when a wider theory is required to explain the relationship of the parts in the complex.

Nagel's discussion clearly shows mechanists do not mean organisms are aggregates by M-1; they mean organisms are parts in interrelation. Further, it would seem that the empirical evidence is against construing organisms as "sums" as Nagel defines this term. To explain organisms wider theories (T*s) are required; indeed, on the whole such theories are still lacking.[24] This is not to say, however, that biological relations are not reducible to physico-chemical ones. It is quite possible that organisms fail to be "sums," yet T* is a theory which contains only physico-chemical laws.

But a more important point is the nature of T*. The existence of any T* affirms the *potentiality* of any physico-chemical part to behave differently "isolated" than it behaves in a complex it organizes. This is precisely the meaning of O-1 (if O-1 is to make any sense at all). Hence the theses M-1 and O-1 are only apparently contraries.

M-2 vs. O-2:

Claims M-2 and O-2 are generally taken to be theses about predictability. That is, O-2 implies that it is not possible to predict the properties of physico-chemical part i in biological complex C(i,j,k) by having knowledge of the properties of i, j, and k in isolation. Defenders of M-2 bring evidence against O-2.[25] The evidence is, on the whole, against "chemical emergence." It is suggested that defenders of O-2 (and "emergence" generally) must mean that compounds, say, water, have properties not in principle predictable from the properties of their atomic components (hydrogen and oxygen). However this is not the case. The properties of compounds can in principle be predicted from the spectroscopic properties of their constituent atoms.

Let us consider how such a prediction is possible. It is possible because we have a theory which explains how parts behave in a complex, i.e., a theory about the relations of the parts within the complex. Generalization of the possibility of prediction of the kind that is claimed by M-2 (prediction of the behavior of physico-chemical part i in biological complex C(i,j,k) from knowledge of isolated i, j, and k) depends upon the existence of a theory which explains the potential of the physico-chemical parts for relationship in C. This condition for predictability suggests that "full knowledge" of isolated parts includes knowledge of the potential predicates applicable to the part for any biological complex that the physico-chemical part can organize. If this be the meaning of "full knowledge" in thesis M-2, then the organicist must accept M-2 because M-2 becomes trivially true. The behavior of i in C(i,j,k) is surely analyzable from the knowledge as to how i behaves in any complex it can organize.

M-3 vs. O-3:

There is an interpretation of O-3 which renders it logically absurd.[26] The organicist must accept the obvious fact that organisms are organized of physico-chemical parts; hence there is a sense in which the organism is determined by its physico-chemical parts. The only logical meaning of "determine" in O-3 is a reference to the fact that there is modification of physico-chemical part according to the biological complex it organizes.[27] But this amounts to nothing more than the affirmation of the empirical claim that we have seen in discussing M-1 and O-1 and M-2 and O-2 that physico-chemical parts have the potential to behave differently in different complexes they organize. Indeed this kind of behavior is exemplified by physico-chemical parts organizing physico-chemical complexes (the behavior of an "isolated" electron is not the same as its behavior in the hydrogen atom).

The kind of "determination" of physico-chemical part by biological complex is in no way contrary to M-3, if we have correctly stated the meaning of "full understanding" in M-2. In discussions of the mechanist meaning of the *properties* of physico-chemical parts, one finds the following phrases:

(1) "relational properties"[28]
(2) "potential of being fashioned into"[29]
(3) "basic architectonic tendency inherent in the fundamental particles of matter itself"[30]
(4) "inherent power of spontaneous self-assembly"[31]

If properties (1)-(4) be included in a listing of the properties of physico-chemical parts, then clearly there is no real difference in meaning between claims M-2 and O-2; M-3 and O-3. "Full understanding" of physico-chemical parts which includes such properties as (1)-(4) above precludes any possibility of making sense of "in isolation" in O-2, and "determination" of a biological complex by these properties of physico-chemical parts includes "determination" of the physico-chemical parts by the biological complex.

M-4 vs. O-4:

Three preliminary remarks will help to clarify the issues involved in M-4 and O-4.

(1) O-4 cannot mean that organicist biologists do not proceed by the use of analytical methods—i.e., by "concentrating on a limited set of properties things possess and ignoring (at least for a time) others, and by investigating the traits selected for study under controlled conditions."[32]

(2) O-4 cannot mean that there has been no success in biology by using analytical methods.[33]

(3) M-4 cannot mean that there are no conditions under which it will not be necessary to study an organism by methods other than analysis of its physico-chemical parts. In particular, studying the whole organism as well as studying its physico-chemical parts will be necessary when a theory is lacking as to what characteristics are predicable of a physico-chemical part when it organizes the organism.[34]

150

O-4 denies the adequacy of analytical methods because of the complexity and hierarchical nature of organisms. Let us consider each.

The complexity of organisms, on the whole, refers to the inhomogeneity of biological complexes as opposed to the homogeneity of the physico-chemical parts which organize them.[35] That is, the physicochemical parts of organisms can be classified into sets in such a way that sampling will, in general, provide the ground for "good" generalizations. On the other hand while it is possible to find homogeneous classes in biology, such classes are "homogeneous in one respect or a few respects, . . . not homogeneous in all relevant biological respects."[36] Such limited homogeneity precludes the general use of the methods of physics and chemistry. However complexity only entails that the use of these methods could reveal at best rather restricted generalizations.

The hierarchical organization of organisms involves recognizing levels of organization or "stratification of stability"[37] and "vertical relationships."[38] It is the "vertical relationships" which make difficulty for analytical methods in biology. These relationships require a "cooperation" of the levels of physico-chemical parts. This is to say that there are "vertical laws" of organization which are in essence laws of modification —they are laws describing the "determination" of the physico-chemical part by the complex which it organizes.[39] These laws are to be contrasted with "horizontal laws" of the physico-chemical parts, i.e., laws which describe the behavior of "isolated parts" without describing their modification in the various complexes which they can organize. Hence O-4 rejects the adequacy of analytical methods in so far as analysis omits vertical laws. There is a further problem with analysis because vertical relationships suggest the possibility of different analyses at different levels of organization in the same complex. This, it would seem, is the foundation for the claim that more traditional biological methods are valuable in guiding the proper application of the analytical methods of physics and chemistry.[40]

It seems clear, however, that with the existence of a theory containing laws of modification, analysis would not be inadequate from the organicist's point of view. Hence O-4 is pointing to the lack, on the whole, of such theories for organisms, whereas M-4 is referring to the possibility of finding them. O-1-O-4 do not entail that such theories will not be found; nor do O-1- O-4 entail that if such theories are found, they will not be expressed in physico-chemical terms and relations. Hence there seems to be no disagreement in principle between M-4 and O-4.

The explication of M-1-M-4 shows that the senses in which organisms (1) are sums of their physico-chemical parts, (2) can be understood by a full understanding of their physico-chemical parts, (3) are determined by their physico-chemical parts, and (4) can be adequately studied by analytical methods depends upon the existence of "full knowledge" of physico-chemical parts in terms of a theory or theories describing the potentiality of these parts to behave differently in different organisms of which they are parts. When this sense of "full knowledge" is understood, the organicist is in agreement with the mechanistic theses M-1-M-4. There is agreement because such full knowledge is implicitly affirming the internal relatedness of parts and whole in the organism. The full knowledge includes knowledge of the relational properties of parts, knowledge of the modification of parts in forming various wholes, and hence knowledge of the reciprocal relationship of whole and parts in the organism.

Then it is clear that "full knowledge" of the parts is sufficient for the deduction of the properties of wholes (higher levels of a hierarchy) from the properties of parts (lower levels of a hierarchy) because "full knowledge" includes knowledge of the whole and its influence on the parts. "Full knowledge" of parts must suffice for the deduction, because it includes the knowledge of the modification of parts in wholes. There is, then, a sense in which the part-whole relationship of organisms can be understood in terms of deducibility, but it is a trivial one; i.e., any view must accept this kind of deducibility because to deny that " 'full knowledge' of parts suffices to deduce the properties of wholes" is a contradiction when "full knowledge" of parts includes a knowledge of a whole by including knowledge of modification of parts by the whole. However there is no significant sense in which one science or theory is reducible to another by such a deduction. A formal reduction, in the organic view, is possible, but not meaningful.

The necessity of this sense of "full knowledge" for the possibility of a deduction, on the other hand, affirms the reciprocal relation between whole and part which is at the foundation of the organic view. This shows that in accepting an interpretation of M-1-M-4 the mechanism which is agreed to by the organicist is "organic mechanism," as described in section 7 of this work.

37. The unity of nature: teleological explanation

The last section considered one of the two criteria generally used to distinguish biology from the physical sciences, *viz.,* that biology studies organic unities (wholes involving modification of parts according to the plan of the whole), whereas the physical sciences study machines (wholes whose properties and behavior result from the properties and behavior of parts).[41] We have seen that this is not a sharp distinction. The explication of how the activities of a whole result from those of its parts involves an affirmation of the nature of physico-chemical entities as organic unities. The second criterion will be considered in this section: the use of teleological explanation in biology in a fundamental way that does not occur in the physical sciences.[42] Teleological explanation has been thought to be necessary for biology because organisms are "goal-directed" in the sense that they exhibit adaptive activities.[43]

The necessity of teleological explanation for biology has been questioned by the formalist tradition. We have seen that the ideal of explanation for the formalists is the deductive model. Many attempts have been made to incorporate teleological explanation into the deductive model. Indeed such an incorporation is necessary if there is to be a formal reduction of biology to physics and chemistry. The basic line of argumentation is to subsume biological "goal-directed" systems under the wider category of "directively organized" systems which can apply to both living and inorganic systems.[44]

"Directive organization" is explained in the following way.[45] Let S represent a system, E the external environment of S, and G a state, property, or behavior belonging to S or potentially belonging to S. Let E remain constant and let S be analyzable into parts or processes x, y, z, with states A_x, B_y, C_z, causally related to G which have permissible values K_A, K_B, K_C, falling within a restricted range K. If S has the property G, or is in a G-state, a change in one of the states (say A) will generally remove S from the G-state. Such a change is called a "primary

153

variation" in S.[46] However if the "primary variation" is accompanied by variations in the other state variables in such a way that S is maintained in the G-state, then the variations of B and C are called "adaptive variations" with respect to the "primary variation."[47]

This analysis can be extended to an environment which is not constant. A changing environment represents an additional factor causally relevant to G. Let the state of E be F_w; then the state of S' $(S+E)$ which is causally relevant to G in S, depends upon the extended matrix (A_x, B_y, C_z, F_w) rather than (A_x, B_y, C_z). The basic difference is that the environment does not in general vary with changes in the internal parts of S—(A, B, C).[48]

This description of "directive organization" is intended to distinguish those systems which are goal-directed from those which are not, but applies to both living and inorganic systems.

The question arises as to the role of teleological explanation in the organic view. Is teleological explanation a criterion for distinguishing biology from the physical sciences because it is a requirement for the explanation of living but not inorganic organisms? We have seen that Whitehead clearly stressed teleology in demarcating life (section 8). In all major discussions of the concept of "living" in PR, AI, and MT, the notion of "aim" appears as a criterion for the living as opposed to the inorganic:

(1) An organism is 'alive' when in some measure its reactions are inexplicable by *any* tradition of pure physical inheritance.

Explanation by 'tradition' is merely another phraseology for explanation by 'efficient cause.' We require explanation by 'final cause.' Thus a single occasion is alive when the subjective aim which determines its process of concrescence has introduced a novelty of definiteness not to be found in the inherited data of its primary phase. The novelty is introduced conceptually and disturbs the inherited 'responsive' adjustment of subjective forms (PR 159).

(2) Those activities in the self-formation of actual occasions which, if coordinated, yield living societies are the intermediate mental functionings transforming the initial phase of reception into the final phase of anticipation. In so far as the mental spontaneities of occasions do not thwart each other, but are directed to a common objective amid varying circumstances, there is life. The essence of life is the teleological introduction of novelty, with some conformation of objectives. Thus novelty of circumstance is met with novelty of functioning adapted to steadiness of purpose (AI 266).

154

(3) We must add yet another character to our description of life. This missing characteristic is 'aim'. By this term 'aim' is meant the exclusion of the boundless wealth of alternative potentiality, and the inclusion of that definite factor of novelty which constitutes the selected way of entertaining those data in that process of unification. The aim is at that complex of feeling which is the enjoyment of those data in that way. 'That way of enjoyment' is selected from the boundless wealth of alternatives. It has been aimed at for actualization in that process (MT 207-08).

These passages describe the adaptation of societies in terms of a stimulus-response situation. Living societies have a wider range of possible responses than inorganic ones. The three passages describe the nature of these responses. Recall that societies are organisms in the sense of section 8 of this work. The description of adaptation of societies is therefore applicable to organisms.

The passage from PR is the simplest statement. In inorganic organisms a particular stimulus S is the efficient cause of a particular response R. In living organisms the same stimulus causally relevant to R can evoke a different response R_1 by virtue of other relevant causal factors which are final rather than efficient causes.

The distinction between living and inorganic organisms is further elucidated in (2). Here it is claimed that the stimulus-response situation of inorganic organisms is not as simple as the description in (1). Rather final causes are potentially causally relevant in the determination of the response of inorganic organisms, but are rendered ineffective because they cancel or "average" out one another. Hence stimulus S results in response R. In living organisms, on the other hand, the multiplicity of final causes is canalized in such a way that a causally relevant final cause is effective in producing response R_1.

Finally (3) describes a still more complex situation in the responses of living organisms to stimuli. Not all the possible final causes can be causally effective. Some are excluded; others are included. The ones included are capable of being canalized into an effective final cause in the production of the response.

The question arises as to whether the role of final causes in the determination of a response to a stimulus constitutes a necessary factor in the explanation of living but not inorganic organisms. Or, is the adaptive response of living organisms capable of being subsumed under a sense of adaptation applicable also to inorganic organisms (as both living and inorganic systems can be "directively organized")?

We have seen (section 12) that inorganic organisms survive in the fact of a changing environment in two fundamental ways: by specialization according to the pattern of the environment and by averaging out the diverse final causes. Both reactions constitute adaptation of an organism to its wider social environment. The organism is becoming more fit in both cases. These kinds of adaptation tend to appear as responses which are sheerly repetitive ones, based solely on an initial stimulus. However the stimulus is far more complex; it involves reenactment of the past, but it also involves information from the wider social environment itself—information about the response the organism is to make if it is to survive. In the sense that the social environment is sending information about survival to the inorganic organism, teleology is involved. Survival depends upon adaptation, and adaptation, in turn, depends upon final causes whose locus is in the sustaining social environment itself.

For living organisms information necessary for survival also comes from the wider social environment. In living organisms, however, there is an ability to include/exclude and to canalize that which is included in order to produce responses which are more than sheerly repetitive. However the responses cannot be novel without limit. The responses must be within the range of the sustaining inorganic environmental order which protects every living organism. Not any response is appropriate; some living species become extinct.

That the pattern of teleological adaptation applies to both living and inorganic organisms is also seen in the doctrine that both inorganic and living organisms evolve. The factor most causally relevant to evolution is novelty in responses to stimuli. To evolve, then, the inorganic organisms must be capable of some novelty of response; specialization and averaging out are not mechanisms which lead to evolutionary development.

There is, then, no special kind of explanation required for living, but not inorganic, organisms. Both are adaptive in a sense that requires the functioning of final causes. The explanation of both is teleological in this fundamental sense.

There is a unity in nature in the sense that there is no sharp distinction between the explanation of the living and the inorganic. This

156

affirms the general model of reciprocal fitness of organism and environment discussed in section 11 of this work. The fitness of the environment is an order of an environment allowing more particular orders to be sustained and to evolve. The fitness of organisms consists in their potential to adapt to specific environmental orders. Living organisms clearly survive, adapt, and evolve. Yet the physico-chemical constituents of living organisms which are ordinarily conceived to be the environment of organisms also survive, adapt, and evolve and thus can be considered inorganic organisms to a more general inorganic environment. Survival, adaptation, and evolution apply both to the living and the inorganic.

The examination of the possibility of formal reduction in the organic view has shown that the reduction of one theory or science to another and the prediction of properties of higher levels of a hierarchically structured whole from properties of lower levels are not distinct issues. An explication of the deduction of properties of wholes from constituents has shown that such a deduction can be made but is not significant. An examination of the modes of explanation in biology and in the physical sciences has shown the explanations to be reducible to one generic kind, a mode always involving teleology. Hence the doctrine that "all sciences study organisms" leads not to an affirmation of reduction as traditionally conceived, but to an affirmation of the unity of nature based on an underlying sameness of organization and of explanatory principles.

Notes

Introduction

1. See especially Victor Lowe, *Understanding Whitehead* (Baltimore: The Johns Hopkins Press, 1962), pp. 123-296.

2. *Ibid.,* pp. 59-89. See also Laurence Bright, *Whitehead's Philosophy of Physics* (London: Sheed and Ward, 1958) and Robert Palter, *Whitehead's Philosophy of Science* (Chicago: University of Chicago Press, 1960).

3. W. Mays, *The Philosophy of Whitehead* (London: George Allen and Unwin, Ltd., 1959), p. 20.

4. Nathaniel Lawrence, *Whitehead's Philosophical Development: A Critical History of the Background of Process and Reality* (Berkeley: University of California Press, 1956).

5. Lowe, *Understanding Whitehead,* p. 84.

6. *Ibid.,* pp. 227-28.

7. Palter, *Whitehead's Philosophy of Science,* p. 1.

8. Ivor Leclerc, *Whitehead's Metaphysics: An Introductory Exposition* (London: George Allen and Unwin, Ltd., 1958), p. ix.

9. *Ibid.,* pp. 3-5.

10. *Ibid.,* p. 5.

11. Palter, *Whitehead's Philosophy of Science,* Ch. 3.

12. *Ibid.,* p. 22; Lowe, *Understanding Whitehead,* p. 62.

Chapter I

1. "Region" is not used here in the special sense of PR but, rather, as roughly equivalent to the use of "volume" by Lowe. See Lowe, *Understanding Whitehead,* Ch. 8.

2. Axioms (2) and (3) entail the thesis that there are no minimum or maximum events. Whitehead later modified this thesis and recognized minimally extended events in nature.

3. See the discussions of Lowe, *Understanding Whitehead,* Ch. III, sec. 4, and Palter, *Whitehead's Philosophy of Science,* Ch. VI.

4.

5.

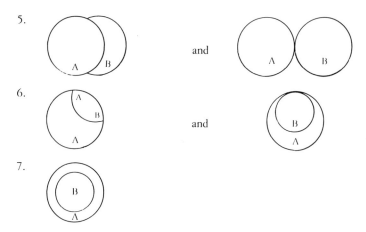

6.

and

7.

8. Note that this is the definition of a line segment. A *straight* line segment requires the additional concept of an ovate class of regions. See PR, Part IV, Ch. III.

9. We will use the terms "actual entities" and "actual occasions" indifferently in our discussion.

10. The distinction is between eternal objects as pure potentials, i.e., as having a general capacity for determination and eternal objects as realized determinants, i.e., as the determinations of the definiteness of particular actual entities.

11. For an illuminating discussion, see Ivor Leclerc, "Whitehead and the Theory of Form," in *Process and Divinity; The Hartshorne Festschrift*, ed. W. L. Reese and E. Freeman (La Salle, Ill.: The Open Court Publishing Co., 1964), pp. 127-37.

12. By a "nexus," Whitehead understands two or more actual occasions concretely and definitely in relation. "Actual entities involve each other by reason of their prehensions of each other. There are thus real individual facts of the togetherness of actual entities, which are real, individual, and particular, in the same sense in which actual entities and the prehensions are real, individual, and particular. Any such particular fact of the togetherness among actual entities is called a 'nexus' (plural form is written 'nexūs')" (PR 29-30).

Chapter III

1. Baldwin, James Mark, ed., *Dictionary of Philosophy and Psychology*, Vol. II (New York: The Macmillan Co., 1911), p. 218.

2. This "averaging out" is described as a survival mechanism in PR. See pp. 154-55.

3. This sense of "environment" is reflected in contemporary ecological writings. (a) is reflected in the thesis that entities are not passive but actively influence their environment. "Organisms are not just passive actors in a physical and chemical milieu, but are active participants in the regulation of their own environment. No

one organism or population alone has much control, of course, but the sum total of processes in the well-ordered ecosystem ensures continuous supplies of materials and energy needed for life." Eugene P. Odum, *Ecology* (New York: Holt, Rinehart and Winston, 1963), p. 56. (b) is reflected in the thesis that communities are "expressions of environment": "Briefly, he [Darwin] suggested that there are throughout nature two inherent traits in living organisms—a tendency to vary and a capacity to increase beyond the means of survival. Some variations are better suited to the conditions of the environment than others. Organisms with favorable variations tend to survive, those without tend to disappear. This process he called Natural Selection with environment serving as the selective screen. Thus life as we know it has not only become adjusted to its many environments, but is an expression of environment as well as its own innate tendencies." Paul B. Sears, *Where There Is Life* (New York: Dell Publishing Co., 1962), p. 72.

4. This sense of "environment" is reflected in the notion that anything relevant to sustaining life is part of its environment. Hence the biosphere is referred to as man's environment. See G. Evelyn Hutchinson, "The Biosphere," in *The Biosphere* (San Francisco: W. H. Freeman and Co., 1970), p. 3. At the same time "environment" can refer to more limited conditions or structures relevant to sustaining organisms. See J. W. Stork and L. P. W. Renouf, *Plant and Animal Ecology* (London: John Murray, 1933), Ch. VII, "The Organism Itself as the Environment." In this chapter Stork and Renouf discuss "organisms themselves" as "the determining factor upon which the presence or absence of organisms depends;" i.e., in the cases of epiphytes and epizootics, commensulism, symbiosis, and parasitism.

5. This sense of "environment" is reflected in the difficulty ecologists have in setting limits to an environment. "This external world is the environment in which organisms live—or is it? I suppose we might define the environment in three different ways: as including only the elements perceived by the organism; as including all elements which affect the organism, whether perceived or not; or as including all elements that can be detected or inferred, whether they influence the organism in any way or not. We might call the first the perceptual environment of an organism; the second, the effective environment; while the third, I suppose, is the total reality that worries the philosophical mind." Marston Bates, *The Forest and the Sea* (New York: Random House, 1960), p. 179.

6. See, for example, D. C. Phillips, "Organicism in the Late Nineteenth and Early Twentieth Centuries," *Journal of the History of Ideas* 31 (1970): 416.

7. This is quite similar to D. Bohm's distinction of immediate and background causes, *Causality and Chance in Modern Physics* (London: Routledge and Kegan Paul, Ltd., 1957), pp. 9-10:

> In order to deal with the problems raised by our inability to know all of the significant causal factors that may contribute to a given effect, there has evolved a distinction between immediate causes and conditions (or background causes). The immediate causes may be defined as those which, when subjected to the changes that take place in a given context, will produce a significant change in

161

the effects. The conditions may be defined as those factors which are necessary for the production of the results in question, but which do not change sufficiently in the context of interest to produce an appreciable change in the effects. For example, one might say that fertile soil plus plenty of rainfall provides the general conditions (or background) needed for the growth of good crops. But the immediate cause would be the planting of the appropriate seeds.

The distinction between immediate causes and conditions is, however, an abstraction, useful for analysis but not strictly correct. For the background can always be changed, provided that conditions are altered sufficiently. We have seen, for example, in the case of the investigation of the cause of beri-beri, the origin of this disease had been confused by the existence of a general background in which most foods had enough vitamins for an adequate diet. But later investigations disclosed conditions in which this background did not exist.

Not only can background conditions be changed by external factors, but very often they can be changed significantly, after enough time, by the processes taking place in the background itself. For example, the cutting down of forests followed by the planting of crops may exhaust the fertility of the soil, and may change the climate and the annual rainfall appreciably. In physics, the influence of any process on its "background" is even more strikingly brought out by Newton's Law that action and reaction are equal. From this law, it follows that it is impossible for any one body to affect another without itself being affected in some measure. Thus, in reality no perfectly constant background can exist. Nevertheless, in any given problem a large number of factors may remain constant enough to permit them to be regarded, to an adequate degree of approximation, as forming a constant background. Thus the distinction between immediate causes and conditions, or background causes, is relative and dependent on the conditions. Yet, because we can never be sure that we have included *all* of the significant causes in our theory, all causal laws must always be completed by specifying the conditions or background in which we have found that they are applicable.

8. I do not think this meaning is essentially different from D. Bohm's use of "background" and "substructure," *Causality and Change in Modern Physics,* p. 138f.

Chapter IV

1. *The Fitness of the Environment* (New York: The Macmillan Co., 1913); *The Order of Nature* (Cambridge, Mass.: Harvard University Press, 1917); *Blood* (Cambridge, Mass.: Harvard University Press, 1928), Ch. 1.

2. Henderson, "The Functions of an Environment," *Science* 39 (1914): 524-27. This article is Henderson's own summary of *The Fitness of the Environment.*

3. Henderson, "The Functions of an Environment," pp. 524-25.

4. It is interesting to note that Henderson takes this to be the definition of "mechanism." "It seems to be true . . . that with the progress of science the term

mechanism has come to mean merely any active system. . . . According to this definition the mechanistic explanation of a phenomenon is simply its explanation as the activity of a system. . . ." ("The Functions of an Environment," p. 526). It is reasonable to believe that "mechanism" as Whitehead used the term in the phrase "organic mechanism" is close to Henderson's meaning.

5. Henderson, "The Functions of an Environment," p. 527.

6. *Ibid.*

7. Henderson, *The Fitness of the Environment,* p. 299.

8. *Ibid.,* pp. 299-300.

9. Henderson, *The Order of Nature,* p. iii.

10. *Ibid.,* p. iv.

11. *Ibid.*

12. Whitehead distinguishes a subordinate society from a subordinate nexus in a structured society in the following way: a subordinate society could retain its dominant feature in a more general environment without the structured society; the order of a subordinate nexus could not be sustained without the structured society as its environment. (PR 152)

13. Henderson, *Blood,* pp. 20-21.

Chapter V

1. Whitehead suggests other mechanisms for the survival of highly complex organisms: "(i) elimination of diversities of detail, and (ii) origination of novelties of conceptual reaction" (PR 154-157). The efficiency of these more special mechanisms depends on the more general mechanisms suggested in SMW.

Chapter VI

1. Gerard Radnitzky, *Contemporary Schools of Meta-science* (Chicago: Henry Regnery Co., 1973), p. xvi.

2. *Ibid.,* p. 20. Radnitzky includes Carnap, Feigl, and Hempel in this group as well as "Quine qua philosopher of science."

3. *Ibid.,* pp. 20-21.

4. *Ibid.,* p. 21. Radnitzky considers Bergman to be a member of this group as well as "Quine qua ontologist."

5. *Ibid.* This group includes Popper and his followers: Albert, Agassi, Feyerabend, Watkins, Lakatos.

6. *Ibid.,* p. 22. Radnitzky distinguishes three subgroups: (1) the pragmatists Dewey, Charles Morris, Churchman, Holzkamp; (2) the pragmatist Pierce; and (3) the praxiologists Kotarbinski and Lange.

7. T. Kisiel and G. Johnson, "New Philosophies of Science in the USA," *Zeitschrift für allgemeine Wissenschaftstheorie,* 5 (1974): 138-89.

8. *Ibid.,* p. 138.

9. H. Putnam, "What Theories are Not," in *Logic, Methodology, and Philosophy of Science: Proceedings of the 1960 International Congress,* ed. Nagel, Suppes, and Tarski (Stanford: Stanford University Press, 1962); F. Suppe, "The Search for Philosophic Understanding of Scientific Theories," in *The Structure of Scientific Thought,* ed. F. Suppe (Urbana, Ill.: University of Illinois Press, 1974), pp. 3-241.

10. Mary B. Hesse, *The Structure of Scientific Inference* (London: The Macmillan Co., 1974), pp. 1-8; Popper, "Normal Science and its Dangers," in *Criticism and the Growth of Knowledge,* ed. Lakatos and Musgrave (Cambridge: Cambridge University Press, 1970), pp. 51-58.

11. For example, H. Feigl, Carl Hempel, Karl Popper, and Ernest Nagel.

12. For example, P. K. Feyeraband, T. S. Kuhn, S. Toulmin, and N. R. Hanson. Although Hanson wrote about a "logic of discovery," his view fits within the framework of historical relativism. See his "The Idea of a Logic of Discovery," in *What I Do Not Believe, and Other Essays,* ed. S. Toulmin and H. Woolf (Dordrecht: Reidel, 1971) pp. 288-300.

13. Hesse, *The Structure of Scientific Inference,* pp. 6-7.

14. I am referring to Karl Popper and his followers. See *The Logic of Scientific Discovery* (London: Hutchinson and Co., Ltd., 1959), sections 4, 6, and 85.

15. Popper, *The Logic of Scientific Discovery,* section 4.

16. T. S. Kuhn and his followers. See *The Structure of Scientific Revolutions* (Chicago: University of Chicago Press, 1970).

17. P. K. Feyeraband and his followers. See especially "How to Be a Good Empiricist," in *Philosophy of Science: The Delaware Seminar,* vol. 2, ed. B. Baumrin (New York: Interscience Publishers, 1963), pp. 3-39; and "Consolations for the Specialist," in *Criticism and the Growth of Knowledge,* ed. Lakatos and Musgrave (Cambridge: Cambridge University Press, 1970), pp. 197-230.

18. See Feyeraband's definition in "How to Be a Good Empiricist": "Metaphysical systems are scientific theories in their most primitive stage" (p. 34).

Chapter VII

1. See, for example, discussions by Hempel, *Philosophy of Natural Science* (Englewood Cliffs, N. J.: Prentice-Hall, Inc., 1966), pp. 54-58; E. Nagel, *The Structure of Science* (New York: Harcourt, Brace, and World, Inc., 1961), Ch. 4.

2. See, for example, C. G. Hempel and P. Oppenheim, "The Logic of Explanation," *Philosophy of Science* 15 (1948): 156. P. Achinstein accepts a modified version of this criterion, *Law and Explanation* (Oxford: Clarendon Press, 1971), p. 30f.

3. Hempel and Oppenheim, "The Logic of Explanation," p. 156. E. Nagel, *The Structure of Science,* p. 59 and P. Achinstein, *Law and Explanation,* pp. 26-27, accept modified versions.

4. Hempel, *Philosophy of Natural Science,* p. 56; Nagel, *The Structure of Science,* pp. 68-72.

5. Hempel, *Philosophy of Natural Science,* p. 56; Nagel, *The Structure of Science,*

pp. 68-72; P. Achinstein, *Law and Explanation,* pp. 49-53; R. Chisholm, "The Contrary-to-fact Conditional," *Mind* 55 (1946): 289-303; N. Goodman, "The Problem of Counter-factual Conditionals," *Journal of Philosophy* 44 (1947): 113-26.

6. Aspects of this criterion are supported by the following: J. J. C. Smart, *Between Science and Philosophy* (New York: Random House, 1968), pp. 63-64; P. Achinstein, *Law and Explanation,* pp. 46-48; M. Scriven, "The Key Property of Physical Laws—Inaccuracy," in M. Feigl and G. Maxwell, eds., *Current Issues in the Philosophy of Science* (New York: Holt, Rinehart and Winston, 1961), p. 100; A. Pap, *An Introduction to the Philosophy of Science* (New York: Free Press, 1963), pp. 301-05; R. B. Braithwaite, *Scientific Explanation* (Cambridge: Cambridge University Press, 1953), p. 11.

7. S. Toulmin, *Philosophy of Science* (London: Hutchinson and Co., Ltd., 1953), Ch. 2.

8. J. J. C. Smart, *Philosophy and Scientific Realism* (London: Humanities Press, 1963), pp. 52-57, and *Between Science and Philosophy,* p. 92f. See also J. D. Bernal, "Molecular Structure, Biochemical Function, and Evolution," in T. Waterman and M. Morowitz, eds., *Theoretical and Mathematical Biology* (New York: Blaisdell Publishing Co., 1965), p. 97; J. Bronowski, "New Concepts in the Evolution of Complexity," *Synthese* 21 (1970): 235-36.

9. Robert Ackermann, "Mechanism, Methodology, and Biological Theory," *Synthese* 20 (1969): 222-23.

10. For critical discussions of (1), see J. J. C. Smart, *Between Science and Philosophy,* pp. 59-62; Nagel, *The Structure of Science,* pp. 57-58; P. Achinstein, *Law and Explanation,* pp. 30-35. For discussions of (2), see Nagel, *The Structure of Science,* pp. 59f; Pap, *An Introduction to the Philosophy of Science,* pp. 292-95. For discussions of (3) and (4), see Smart, *Between Science and Philosophy,* p. 62f; Scriven, "The Key Property," p. 100; Pap, *An Introduction to the Philosophy of Science,* pp. 289-92. For a discussion of (5), see M. Simon, *The Matter of Life* (New Haven: Yale University Press, 1971), p. 13.

11. See discussions by Bohm, *Causality and Chance in Modern Physics,* p. 138f; and Whitehead, PR, p. 138f.

12. Nagel, *The Structure of Science,* p. 59.

13. Achinstein, *Law and Explanation,* pp. 26-27.

14. *Ibid.*

15. *Ibid.,* p. 26.

16. See, for example, W. Kneale, "Natural Laws and Counter-to-Fact Conditionals," *Analysis* 10 (1950): 123.

17. Consider Kneale's discussion, and Nagel's discussion, *The Structure of Science,* pp. 68-69, of the failure of "All ravens are black" to support a subjunctive conditional. We do not believe in the support because we know it is possible that the color of ravens may be affected by environmental conditions existing in regions other than those in which ravens are presently found, say, polar regions. The case is not different for the rusty screws in Smith's present car. The truth of the subjunctive

conditional involves a wider environment than the conditions of Smith's present car, and we believe the conditions of this wider environment to be sufficiently different to allow the existence of nonrusty screws.

18. Achinstein, *Law and Explanation*, pp. 49-54; Nagel, *The Structure of Science*, pp. 68-73; Pap, *An Introduction to the Philosophy of Science*, pp. 289-92; N. Rescher, "Belief-contravening Suppositions," *Philosophical Review* 70 (1961): 176-96.

19. Pap, *An Introduction to the Philosophy of Science*, p. 302.

20. A frequently discussed example is the postulation of the existence of the neutrino to "save" the law of conservation of energy confronted with the phenomenon of beta-ray decay. See Nagel, *The Structure of Science*, p. 65 and Achinstein, *Law and Explanation*, p. 46.

21. Achinstein, *Law and Explanation*, pp. 46-47.

22. *Ibid.*, p. 47.

23. See discussions by Nagel, *The Structure of Science*, pp. 64-66 and Achinstein, *Law and Explanation*, pp. 46-49.

24. Nagel, *The Structure of Science*, p. 66.

25. Smart, *Between Science and Philosophy*, p. 93: "An exception to a generalization of natural history is scientifically harmless: it merely leads us to change 'all' to 'nearly all'. Thus the generalization that all animals which suckle their young do not lay eggs has had to be changed simply to the generalization that all animals which suckle their young, except for the platypus and the echidna, do not lay eggs."

26. It seems that Kuhn would be in agreement with the main points of Toulmin's discussion: (1) that laws are formal principles, (2) that laws are not true or false, and (3) that the function of laws is in drawing inferences. In the "Postscript" to *The Structure of Scientific Revolutions* he categorizes laws as one of the forms of the "symbolic generalizations" to which a scientific community is committed. Although the aim of the discussion is not to ascertain the status of laws, but to clarify the components of shared commitment of a scientific community, it is clear that symbolic generalizations functioning as laws of nature are formal principles. They are "expressions . . . which can readily be cast in a logical form like $(x)(y)(z)$ $()$ (x,y,z). They are the formal or the readily formalizable components of the disciplinary matrix" (p. 182). It is also clear that Kuhn is not maintaining "true" or "false" to be relevant to the characterization of laws. To do so would contradict the thesis of Chapter XIII—that there is no progress toward truth in science. Finally symbolic generalizations functioning as laws of nature are used for drawing inferences: "If it were not for the general acceptance of expressions like these, there would be no points at which group members could attach the powerful techniques of logical and mathematical manipulation in their puzzle-solving enterprise" (p. 183).

27. S. Toulmin, *Human Understanding*, I (Princeton: Princeton University Press, 1972), pp. 168-69.

28. Toulmin, *Human Understanding*, I, pp. 168-71. This does not differ from his earlier discussion of laws in *Philosophy of Science*, Ch. 3.

29. Toulmin, *Philosophy of Science*, pp. 77-78.

30. *Ibid.*, pp. 50-53.

31. *Ibid.*, p. 78.

32. *Ibid.*, p. 69 and p. 101.

33. *Ibid.*, pp. 98-100. Toulmin explicitly states that he is following Kneale's interpretation of Whitehead. See W. Kneale, *Probability and Induction* (Oxford: Clarendon Press, 1949), pp. 72-73.

34. I take Bohm to hold a position on laws very similar to that put forward as the organic view. He discusses laws as restricted, as essentially statistical in character, and as capable of evolving. See *Causality and Chance in Modern Physics*, pp. 137-40 and pp. 146-52, and "Some Remarks on the Notion of Order," in *Towards a Theoretical Biology*, 2, *Sketches*, ed. C. H. Waddington (Edinburgh: Edinburgh University Press, 1969), pp. 18-40.

Chapter VIII

1. Hempel, *Philosophy of Natural Science*, p. 14.

2. *Ibid.*, pp. 14-15.

3. *Ibid.*, p. 15.

4. *Ibid.*, p. 18.

5. Popper, *The Logic of Scientific Discovery*, Ch. 1 and *Conjectures and Refutations* (London: Routledge and Kegan Paul, 1963), p. 47.

6. Gary Gutting has referred to this circularity: "In particular I think Whitehead's hypothetico-deductive version of metaphysical method makes him very liable to the charge of circularity in his attempt to justify induction." "Metaphysics and Induction —Rejoinder to James W. Felt, S.J.," *Process Studies* 1 (1971): 181-82. However I do not think Whitehead's method can be characterized as hypothetico-deductive. Section 25 below suggests an inductive logic of hypothesis formation.

7. Nelson Goodman, *Fact, Fiction, and Forecast* (Cambridge, Mass.: Harvard University Press, 1955), p. 68.

8. For example Popper.

9. Toulmin, *The Philosophy of Science*, pp. 20-21.

10. *Ibid.*, p. 21.

11. *Ibid.*, p. 20.

12. N. R. Hanson, *Patterns of Discovery* (Cambridge: Cambridge University Press, 1958), Ch. 1; Kuhn, *The Structure of Scientific Revolutions;* Feyerabend, "How to Be a Good Empiricist."

13. Hanson, *Patterns of Discovery*, p. 10.

14. *Ibid.*, p. 11f.

15. *Ibid.*, p. 19.

16. *Ibid.*, p. 22.

17. Kuhn, *The Structure of Scientific Revolutions*, p. 113.

18. *Ibid.*, p. 15. Hempel and Popper agree with Kuhn that a theory is necessary for determining relevant observations. However their basic rejection of induction is

based upon the justification problem discussed in section 19. See Hempel, *Philosophy of Natural Science,* pp. 11-13; Popper, *Conjectures and Refutations,* pp. 46-47.

19. Feyerabend, "How to Be a Good Empiricist," pp. 19-27.

20. *Ibid.,* p. 35.

21. Mary Hesse, "Consilience of Induction," in *The Problem of Inductive Logic,* ed. I. Lakatos (Amsterdam: North-Holland, 1968), p. 232.

22. *Ibid.,* pp. 232-33.

23. Mary Hesse, "An Inductive Logic of Theories," in *Minnesota Studies in the Philosophy of Science,* IV, ed. Radner and Winokur (Minneapolis: University of Minnesota Press, 1970), p. 164.

24. Carl Hempel, "Studies in the Logic of Confirmation," reprinted in his *Aspects of Scientific Explanation* (New York: The Free Press, 1965), pp. 30-35; Hesse, "An Inductive Logic of Theories," p. 165f; and Hesse, "Positivism and the Logic of Scientific Theories," in *The Legacy of Logical Positivism,* ed. Achinstein and Barker (Baltimore: The Johns Hopkins Press, 1969), p. 97f.

25. Hesse, "An Inductive Logic of Theories," p. 166.

26. Hiliary Putnam, " 'Degree of Confirmation' and Inductive Logic," in *The Philosophy of Rudolf Carnap,* ed. P. A. Schlipp (La Salle, Ill.: The Open Court Publishing Co., 1963), pp. 761-83.

27. Hesse, "Consilience of Inductions," p. 234.

28. *Ibid.,* p. 233.

29. Hesse, "Consilience of Inductions," p. 233f and "An Inductive Logic of Theories," p. 165.

30. Hesse, "An Inductive Logic of Theories," p. 165.

31. *Ibid.,* p. 175.

32. *Ibid.,* p. 166.

33. *Ibid.,* p. 174. See also *The Structure of Scientific Inference,* p. 217.

34. Hesse, "Consilience of Inductions," p. 243. She discusses the prediction of the explosion of the first atomic bomb in terms of her theory, p. 242f.

35. Hesse, "Positivism and the Logic of Scientific Theories," p. 115.

36. The important internal relationship in the "valid inductive inference" pattern is not the relationship of prehension; rather, the relevant internal relations are those between organisms and environmental order. The organisms of an environment contribute to the order and yet cannot exist without that order. The clearest summary of this is, I think, to be found in SMW (215); here Whitehead says anything is "otherwise than what it would have been if placed elsewhere," i.e., if in a different environment. It would be otherwise because the relations between organisms and their environments are internal ones. I do not mean to suggest that environmental order does not depend on prehension for Whitehead. I merely wish to point out that the internal relationship of organism and environment which is required for any "valid induction" may be a doctrine of a metaphysical theory which does not include the doctrine of prehensions.

37. Gutting, "Metaphysics and Induction," *Process Studies* 1 (1971): 177.

38. Hesse, "Positivism and the Logic of Scientific Theories," p. 105.

39. John Maynard Keynes, *A Treatise on Probability* (London: Macmillan and Co., Ltd., 1948), p. 427.

40. *Ibid.,* p. 260.

41.*Ibid.,* p. 249.

42. *Ibid.,* p. 258.

43. *Ibid.,* p. 260; see also Hesse, "Positivism and the Logic of Scientific Theories," p. 105.

44. Keynes, *A Treatise on Probability,* pp. 249-50.

45. *Ibid.,* p. 261.

Chapter IX

1. Nagel, *The Structure of Science,* p. 29.

2. Hempel and Oppenheim, "Studies in the Logic of Explanation," in C. G. Hempel, *Aspects of Scientific Explanation* (New York: Free Press, 1965), pp. 247-51. See also Popper, *The Logic of Scientific Discovery,* sec. 12, and Nagel, *The Structure of Science,* Ch. 2.

3. Hempel and Oppenheim, "Studies in the Logic of Explanation," p. 249.

4. *Ibid.,* pp. 247-48.

5. *Ibid.,* p. 249.

6. Hempel, *Philosophy of Natural Science,* pp. 51-54; "Deductive-Nomological vs. Statistical Explanation," in *Minnesota Studies in the Philosophy of Science,* III, ed. H. Feigl and G. Maxwell (Minneapolis: University of Minnesota Press, 1962), pp. 98-121.

7. Hempel, *Philosophy of Natural Science,* pp. 58-69; "Deductive-Nomological vs. Statistical Explanation," pp. 121-67.

8. Hempel, "Deductive-Nomological vs. Statistical Explanation," p. 121 and p. 128.

9. Hempel, *Philosophy of Natural Science,* p. 67; "Deductive-Nomological vs. Statistical Explanation," p. 121.

10. Hempel and Oppenheim, "Studies in the Logic of Explanation," pp. 251-58.

11. Nagel, *The Structure of Science,* pp. 23-25.

12. See, for example, Hempel, "The Theoretician's Dilemma: A Study in the Logic of Theory Construction," "Empiricist Criterion of Cognitive Significance: Problems and Changes," and "A Logical Appraisal of Operationism," all reprinted in his *Aspects of Scientific Explanation,* pp. 173-226, pp. 101-119, and pp. 123-33, respectively. Also see R. Carnap, "Testability and Meaning," *Philosophy of Science* 3 (1936): 420-468, and Nagel, *The Structure of Science,* pp. 97-105.

13. Feyerabend, "Explanation, Reduction, and Empiricism," in *Minnesota Studies in the Philosophy of Science,* III, pp. 28-97 and "How to Be a Good Empiricist;" Hesse, *The Structure of Scientific Inference,* Ch. 1 and "Positivism and the Logic of Scientific Theories;" W. Shea, "Beyond Logical Empiricism," *Dialogue* 10 (1971): 223-42.

14. Feyerabend, "How to Be a Good Empiricist," p. 10.

15. Feyerabend, "Explanation, Reduction, and Empiricism," p. 95.

16. Toulmin, *Human Understanding,* I, p. 156.

17. *Ibid.,* p. 157.

18. *Ibid.,* p. 158.

19. *Ibid.,* p. 166.

20. *Ibid.,* p. 172.

21. Toulmin uses both the terms "paradigm" and "Ideal of Natural Order." The former is the term used by other historical relativists.

22. Toulmin, *Human Understanding,* I, pp. 172-73.

23. A. N. Whitehead, "The Organization of Thought," reprinted in *The Interpretation of Science* (New York: The Bobbs-Merrill Co., Inc., 1961), p. 21.

24. M. Black, *Models and Metaphors* (Ithaca, N. Y.: Cornell University Press, 1962), pp. 25-47 and pp. 219-43; M. Hesse, "The Explanatory Function of Metaphor," reprinted in her *Models and Analogies in Science* (Notre Dame, Ind.: University of Notre Dame Press, 1966), pp. 157-77.

25. Hesse, "The Explanatory Function of Metaphor."

26. Black, *Models and Metaphors,* pp. 25-47.

27. Hesse, "The Explanatory Function of Metaphor," p. 158.

28. *Ibid.,* p. 162.

29. *Ibid.,* p. 163.

30. *Ibid.,* p. 165.

31. *Ibid.,* pp. 174-75.

32. *Ibid.,* p. 176. In general there are extreme difficulties on the deductivist account of explanation in accounting for prediction in this strong sense. This is due to the fact that new observation predicates can only be added by the correspondence rules. Hesse has argued that there is no rational way to do this. See Mary Hesse, "Theories, Dictionaries, and Observations," *British Journal For the Philosophy of Science.* 9 (1958): 12-28.

33. Hesse, "The Explanatory Function of Metaphor," p. 171.

34. See H. Feigl, "The 'Orthodox' View of Theories: Remarks in Defense as Well as Critique," in *Minnesota Studies in the Philosophy of Science,* IV, ed. Radner and Winokur (Minneapolis: University of Minnesota Press, 1970), pp. 11-12.

35. Hesse, *The Structure of Scientific Inference,* p. 212.

36. *Ibid.,* pp. 210-12. See also Hesse, "Consilience of Inductions," pp. 240-41.

37. Hesse, "Consilience of Inductions," p. 245.

38. This is sometimes discussed as the "diaphoric" aspect of a metaphor, which is distinguished from the "epiphoric" aspect, i.e., the analogy. See Earl R. MacCormac, "Meaning Variance and Metaphor," *British Journal for the Philosophy of Science* 22 (1971): 145-59.

39. Hesse, "The Explanatory Function of Metaphor," p. 176.

Chapter X

1. See, for example, Nagel, *The Structure of Science*, p. 83; Hempel, *Philosophy of Natural Science*, pp. 77-82.

2. Nagel, *The Structure of Science*, pp. 81-90.

3. *Ibid.*, pp. 82-83.

4. *Ibid.*, p. 86.

5. *Ibid.*, p. 87.

6. *Ibid.*

7. *Ibid.*, pp. 93-95.

8. See Popper, *The Logic of Scientific Discovery*, sec. 12.

9. Kuhn, *The Structure of Scientific Revolutions.*

10. *Ibid.*, pp. 182-87.

11. *Ibid.*, p. 15.

12. Toulmin, *Human Understanding*, I, p. 121.

13. D. Shapere, "The Structure of Scientific Revolutions," *Philosophical Review* 73 (1964): 390; William Shea, "Beyond Logical Empiricism," p. 234.

14. Shea, "Beyond Logical Empiricism," p. 235; Carl Kordig, "The Comparability of Scientific Theories," *Philosophy of Science* 38 (1971): 469; and Kordig, "The Theory-Ladenness of Observation," *Review of Metaphysics* 24 (1971): 469.

15. P. Achinstein, "On the Meaning of Scientific Terms," *The Journal of Philosophy* 61 (1964): 498-99; MacCormac, "Meaning Variance and Metaphor," p. 145.

16. Shea, "Beyond Logical Empiricism," p. 235; Kordig, "The Theory-Ladenness of Observation," p. 469; Achinstein, "On the Meaning of Scientific Terms," p. 499.

17. Kuhn, *The Structure of Scientific Revolutions*, Ch. 1.

18. *Ibid.*, Chs. 2, 3, and 4.

19. *Ibid.*

20. *Ibid.*, pp. 62-65 and pp. 111-35.

21. *Ibid.*

22. *Ibid.*, Ch. 12.

23. D. Shapere, "Meaning and Scientific Change," in *Mind and Cosmos: Essays in Contemporary Science and Philosophy*, ed. R. G. Colodny (Pittsburgh: University of Pittsburgh Press, 1966), p. 75f.; Toulmin, *Human Understanding*, I, p. 127f.; Achinstein, "On the Meaning of Scientific Terms," p. 508; Kordig, "The Comparability of Scientific Theories," p. 477; MacCormac, "Meaning Variance and Metaphor," p. 146.

24. Achinstein's second paradox: "On the Meaning of Scientific Terms," pp. 498-99.

25. Kuhn, "Reflections on My Critics," in *Criticism and the Growth of Knowledge*, p. 259f.

26. Kuhn, *The Structure of Scientific Revolutions*, pp. 99-102.

27. *Ibid.*, p. 102.

28. *Ibid.*

29. Kuhn, "Reflections on My Critics," p. 275.

30. Kuhn, *The Structure of Scientific Revolutions,* pp. 200-01.

31. Kuhn, "Reflections on My Critics," pp. 266-67.

32. MacCormac, "Meaning Variance and Metaphor."

33. *Ibid.,* p. 152.

34. Kuhn, "Reflections on My Critics," p. 266, fn. 2.

35. *Ibid.,* p. 260.

36. *Ibid.,* p. 261.

37. *Ibid.*

38. *Ibid.,* pp. 261-62.

39. In response to the claim that his view is relativistic, Kuhn refers to an evolutionary metaphor for scientific development. "If you would think of science's developing in the usual evolutionary treelike pattern, then I think it not only possble [sic.], but indeed quite easy, to do the following: design a set of criteria which would permit a neutral observer to say which of two theories for the same aspect of nature was the later (the more evolved) and which was the earlier. In biological evolution such criteria include specialization and articulation; similar criteria will work for science as well. In this sense scientific development is a unidirectional and irreversible process, and that is not a relativistic view." "Discussion of 'Second Thoughts on Paradigms'," in *The Structure of Scientific Theories,* ed. F. Suppe (Urbana: University of Illinois Press, 1974), p. 508. See also *The Structure of Scientific Revolutions,* pp. 205-6, and "Reflections on My Critics," p. 264.

40. Kuhn, "Reflections on My Critics," p. 265.

41. *Ibid.* See also *The Structure of Scientific Revolutions,* pp. 206-07.

42. Kuhn, *The Structure of Scientific Revolutions,* p. 171.

43. See, for example, Nagel, *The Structure of Science,* p. 117.

44. Hesse, *The Structure of Scientific Inference,* p. 290. It should be noted that not all historical relativists are committed to the instrumentalist view. The point is that the realists are committed to a thesis about the cumulative character of science.

45. Hesse, *The Structure of Scientific Inference,* pp. 287-88.

46. Nagel, *The Structure of Science,* pp. 151-52.

47. Hesse, *The Structure of Scientific Inference,* pp. 295-96.

48. See, for example, J. W. N. Watkins, "Against 'Normal Science'," pp. 34-35, and Feyerabend, "Consolations for the Specialist," pp. 205-07, in *Criticism and the Growth of Knowledge.*

Chapter XI

1. Hempel, *Philosophy of Natural Science,* Ch. 8; Nagel, *The Structure of Science,* pp. 336-66.

2. Hempel and Oppenheim, "Studies in the Logic of Explanation," pp. 258-64; Nagel, *The Structure of Science,* pp. 366-74 and pp. 380-97.

3. Hempel, *Philosophy of Natural Science,* p. 102f.; Nagel, *The Structure of*

Science, p. 352f.

4. *Ibid.*

5. Nagel, *The Structure of Science,* p. 354.

6. *Ibid.* See also Hempel, *Philosophy of Natural Science,* p. 103.

7. Hempel and Oppenheim, "Studies in the Logic of Explanation," pp. 258-64; Nagel, *The Structure of Science,* pp. 366-74 and pp. 380-97.

8. C. W. Berenda, "On Emergence and Prediction," *Journal of Philosophy* 50 (1953): 271; Smart, *Philosophy and Scientific Realism,* p. 51.

9. Nagel, *The Structure of Science,* pp. 367-69.

10. For example, see Feyerabend's discussion, "Explanation, Reduction, and Empiricism."

11. Toulmin, *Foresight and Understanding,* Ch. IV.

12. Kuhn, *The Structure of Scientific Revolutions,* pp. 179-80.

13. Toulmin, *Foresight and Understanding,* p. 63.

14. *Ibid.,* pp. 67-71.

15. Kuhn, *The Structure of Scientific Revolutions,* p. 180.

16. Kuhn, "Reflections on My Critics," p. 252.

17. Kuhn, *The Structure of Scientific Revolutions,* p. 190.

18. *Ibid.,* pp. 190-91.

19. Hempel, *Philosophy of Natural Science,* Ch. 8; Nagel, *The Structure of Science,* Chs. 11 and 12.

20. See, for example, E. Laszlo, *The Systems View of the World* (New York: George Braziller, 1972), p. 31, and Laszlo, "Systems and Structures—Toward Bio-Social Anthropology," *Theory and Decision* 2 (1971): 179.

21. Phillips, "Organicism in the Late Nineteenth and Early Twentieth Century," p. 417.

22. Simon, *The Matter of Life,* p. 156.

23. Nagel, *The Structure of Science,* p. 390.

24. Bronowski, "New Concepts in the Evolution of Complexity," pp. 228-46.

25. C. W. Berenda, "On Emergence and Prediction," p. 291; Simon, *The Matter of Life,* p. 155; and Smart, *Philosophy of Scientific Realism,* pp. 51-52.

26. Phillips, "Organicism in the Late Nineteenth and Early Twentieth Century," p. 418; H. Hein, "Molecular Biology vs. Organicism: The Enduring Dispute Between Mechanism and Vitalism," *Synthese* 20 (1969): 241 and 243.

27. See SMW, pp. 115-16 and pp. 215-16; Bohm, "Further Remarks on Order," in *Towards a Theoretical Biology,* 2: *Sketches,* pp. 51-58.

28. Simon, *The Matter of Life,* p. 155.

29. *Ibid.,* p. 156.

30. Hein, "Molecular Biology vs. Organicism," p. 242.

31. *Ibid.,* p. 248.

32. Nagel, *The Structure of Science,* p. 445.

33. J. Monod, *Chance and Necessity* (New York: Alfred A. Knopf, Inc., 1971), pp. 79-80.

34. Nagel, *The Structure of Science,* p. 440.

35. Ackermann, "Mechanism, Methodology, and Biological Theory," pp. 219-22; W. Elsasser, "Synopsis of Organismic Theory," *Journal of Theoretical Biology* 7 (1964): 59.

36. Ackermann, "Mechanism, Methodology, and Biological Theory," p. 222.

37. Bronowski, "New Concepts in the Evolution of Complexity," p. 272.

38. Bohm, "Further Remarks on Order," pp. 51-58; Laszlo, "Systems and Structures—Toward Bio-Social Anthropology," pp. 178-79; Whitehead, SMW, pp. 215-16.

39. Bohm, "Further Remarks on Order," p. 57; Whitehead, SMW, pp. 215-16.

40. Ackermann, "Mechanism, Methodology, and Biological Theory," p. 224; B. Commoner, "In Defense of Biology," *Science* 133 (1961): 1747.

41. Nagel, *The Structure of Science,* p. 401.

42. *Ibid.*

43. *Ibid.,* p. 408.

44. *Ibid.,* pp. 411-22.

45. *Ibid.,* pp. 411-17.

46. *Ibid.,* p. 414.

47. *Ibid.,* p. 415.

48. *Ibid.,* p. 417.

174